Philosophy and History of Education

Philosophy and History of Education

Diverse Perspectives on Their Value and Relationship

Antoinette Errante, Jackie Blount,
and Bruce A. Kimball

ROWMAN & LITTLEFIELD
Lanham • Boulder • New York • London

Published by Rowman & Littlefield
A wholly owned subsidiary of The Rowman & Littlefield Publishing Group, Inc.
4501 Forbes Boulevard, Suite 200, Lanham, Maryland 20706
www.rowman.com

Unit A, Whitacre Mews, 26-34 Stannary Street, London SE11 4AB

Copyright © 2017 by Antoinette Errante, Jackie Blount, and Bruce A. Kimball

All rights reserved. No part of this book may be reproduced in any form or by any electronic or mechanical means, including information storage and retrieval systems, without written permission from the publisher, except by a reviewer who may quote passages in a review.

British Library Cataloguing in Publication Information Available

Library of Congress Cataloging-in-Publication Data Available
ISBN 978-1-4758-2711-8 (cloth : alk. paper)
ISBN 978-1-4758-2712-5 (pbk. : alk. paper)
ISBN 978-1-4758-2713-2 (electronic)

∞™ The paper used in this publication meets the minimum requirements of American National Standard for Information Sciences Permanence of Paper for Printed Library Materials, ANSI/NISO Z39.48-1992.

Printed in the United States of America

In memory of our colleague, Joe Watras, who deftly traveled between history and philosophy of education throughout his long and distinguished career.

Contents

Foreword: Why History? Why Philosophy? Why Both? — ix

Introduction — xiii

I: The Relationship between Philosophical and Historical Study of Education — 1

1. Why Does History Matter to Philosophy? — 3
   Bryan R. Warnick

2. Philosophy, Literature, and Inductive Historiography — 13
   Bruce A. Kimball

3. The Mutual Intellectual Relationship of John Dewey and Ella Flagg Young: *Contributions to Education* Series, 1901–1902 — 27
   Jackie M. Blount

4. Blending the Philosophy and the History of Education: Discussions of the Works of Boyd Bode, Bernard Mehl, and Maxine Greene — 39
   Joseph Watras

5. History as Critique and Source of Ideology in Education: Tucson's Outlawed Mexican American Studies Program — 51
   Thomas M. Falk

6. A Historical Analysis of "Free-Money" Ideology and Ohio State University President George W. Rightmire, 1926–1938 — 63
   Benjamin A. Johnson

II: The Need of Philosophical and Historical Study in Educational Knowledge, Policy, and Practice — 73

7 A Modest Plea for Collaborative History and Philosophy of Education — 75
   Randall Curren and Charles Dorn

8 Educational Practice in Pursuit of Justice Requires Historically Informed and Philosophically Rigorous Scholarship — 87
   Winston C. Thompson

9 The Predicament of Culture and Educational History and Philosophy as Reconciliation: Seeking out the "Disappeared" through Transdisciplinary Engagement — 99
   Antoinette Errante

10 James Bryant Conant, Science, and Science Education: The Uses of History and Philosophy — 111
   Wayne J. Urban and Sarah E. Wever

11 History and Philosophy of Education as "Pre Qualitative" Educational Research — 123
   Samuel D. Rocha

12 The Blurring and Entanglement of Philosophy and Science: A Response — 133
   Patti Lather

Index — 137

About the Editors — 143

About the Contributors — 145

Foreword

Why History? Why Philosophy? Why Both?

Several years ago, I interviewed for a job at an American education school. Glancing up from my vita, where she had circled several items in a menacing shade of red, the dean of the school looked me straight in the eye and asked, "So will your work help us close the 'achievement gap'?"

I blinked and cleared my throat, trying to buy time. The right answer was obviously yes, but it seemed wrong to say that if I didn't believe it. So I said no. Surely, I told the dean, history can illuminate how the achievement gap came to replace integration as our dominant metaphor for thinking and talking about race and education. Fifty years ago, liberal politicians and educators focused their efforts on bringing students of different racial backgrounds into the same classrooms. But today, they more commonly aim to narrow the stark inequalities in educational resources—and, most of all, in educational achievement—across these groups. Historians can certainly document the achievement gap, I said, and we can also explain how it has largely trumped concerns about racial integration in our public discourse. But we can't close it.

I didn't get the job. Looking back, though, I also think I flubbed the question. Of course history can't yield ironclad policy prescriptions, of the X-happened-so-Y-should-happen variety. But history can and should inform the questions we ask about the world we want to inhabit. And historians can surely provide some signposts—if not specific directions—about how to create it, if we align ourselves strategically with other disciplines.

That's where philosophy comes in, as the smart chapters in this book remind us. Philosophers spend their waking hours considering matters of "value," which start with the most essential question of all: what is a good life, and what makes it worth living? So they can help historians—and everyone else—think through the ethical and moral implications of the stories that we unearth and of the ways we choose to tell them.

I learned all of that firsthand while writing a book about the teaching of controversial issues with Emily Robertson for a series that I coedit with Randall Curren. Each volume in the series brings together a historian and a philosopher to examine a hot-button debate in contemporary education. At first, I thought the division of labor would be fairly simple: the historian would tell us how we arrived at our current juncture, and the philosopher would tell us where we should go from here. But as Curren and Charles Dorn note in their contribution to this book, things turned out to be much more complicated than that.

In the course of my discussions with Robertson, I realized that I hadn't examined the question of "controversy" itself. What made an issue truly controversial, as opposed to simply contested? And what are the stakes in the answer? Robertson's careful examination of the "controversy over controversy" helped us produce a book with a much stronger analytic core—and, I think, a much clearer policy perspective—than I could have written on my own. Hopefully, we framed a case for teaching issues that are truly controversial while omitting ones that aren't.

Like the chapters in this book, meanwhile, I also hope we made a case for a certain kind of humanistic inquiry in the study of education writ large. Most education-related scholarship occurs in preprofessional settings, especially schools of education, which have increasingly embraced a kind of latter-day positivism. Spurred in part by No Child Left Behind and the high-stakes testing revolution it unleashed, many ed-schools are focusing their attention—and, of course, their resources—on quantitative experiments to measure and improve learning. That's a good thing—indeed, it's a great thing—so long as we don't lose sight of the broader events, trends, and values that brought us to this moment in the first place.

Historians won't close the achievement gap on their own, as I told the ed-school dean many moons ago, nor can they single-handedly tackle substance abuse, antigay bullying, or any of the other glaring problems that bedevil American education. But working in concert with philosophers, we can cast new light on the nature of these conditions and also suggest some concrete steps for ameliorating them.

This isn't just a matter of widening our intellectual horizons, as per the William James formulation that Bryan Warnick wisely invokes in his contribution to this volume. We can also reveal new paths toward practical solutions, which were previously hidden from our vision, and we can counter our all-too-natural tendency toward cynicism, which limits human improvement as much as human imagination. There aren't any simple answers here, of course, but that doesn't mean we should simply throw up our hands. And cursing the darkness only delays the dawn.

Jonathan Zimmerman
Professor
New York University

Introduction

It would not be difficult to imagine the authors of this volume assembled at a dinner party and playfully ribbing each other about the relative merits of their beloved disciplines:

"Well, it's possible that history might be useful in the service of philosophy . . ."

"By 'in the service,' are you suggesting that history does the grunt work and that philosophy elevates it?"

"Oh, you philosophers just can't be sullied by anything empirical, can you?"

"Well, you historians are all obsessed with facts and acts!"

"You know, there's actually been quite a lot written about history since Nietzsche that might be of interest to you . . ."

"Are you suggesting the social sciences have to DIE in order for the humanities to live?"

As philosophers and historians, we love our chosen disciplines, and while the tensions and debates within as well as between our fields are legion and a time-honored tradition, in this volume, we turn our attention to some of the ways in which, working together, those differences can be productive. Conflicts, after all, are often where things get interesting.

There are many potential sources of disagreement among the points of view—implicit and explicit—offered by authors in this volume: the relative merits of logico-deductive versus inductive reasoning; intuition versus data; what constitutes philosophy or history; the meaning and intellectual origins of concepts such as "ideology" or "indigenous people"; and how our disciplines should relate to other kinds of scholarship such as literature or the social sciences. And always, it seems, Dewey, Dewey, Dewey.

Still, we found that through collaboration those differences presented possibilities for our ancient disciplines to contribute to thoroughly modern perspectives on educational processes, problems, and solutions that are more nuanced than those we could have conjured separately. While we do not believe the authors' perspectives in this volume regarding the relationship and need of philosophy and history of education are exhaustive, we hope they contribute to an ongoing dialogue regarding the possibilities of collaborative philosophical and historical endeavors for the advancement of educational theory and practice.

While most of the chapters in this volume address both the relationship and the need of philosophy and history of education to some extent, we have organized them based upon their broader contribution to the former or latter question. Moreover, just as disciplinary conventions in history, philosophy, feminist studies, social sciences, and other fields vary, the narrative voices adopted by scholars in these fields vary as well. The voices of individual essays in this volume reflect that variation, and we believe that these differences suit the cross-disciplinary nature of this volume.

In the first section of the book, authors attend to the ways in which philosophy and history of education are related. There are two recurring themes in the chapters. First, they suggest that the methods and concerns of history and philosophy of education are somewhat complementary. When put to the service of collaborative work, those aspects of our disciplines about which we most often disagree or tease each other can often bring greater clarity and depth of understanding to a common educational problem of interest.

Whereas philosophy can illuminate the values and beliefs undergirding educational issues and the nature of knowledge, history can provide perspectives on the actors and circumstances that influenced those values and beliefs over time and how their evolution has shaped contemporary educational policies, discourses, and debates. In so doing, historical and philosophical collaboration can reveal not only what is unaccounted for—and in some cases systematically rendered invisible—within our own disciplinary visions but also the unexamined, taken-for-granted aspects of educational problems and issues.

Secondly, authors return time and again to the imaginative and intuitive nature of their work. Historical and philosophical works are not only the sum total of data (however understood) and method. There is an ineffable, mysterious quality to what Bryan Warnick calls the "spark" that guides philosophers' and historians' questions and insights and the ways in which they identify the salient details of their work. Indeed, history and philosophy provide that spark for each other more often than we generally acknowledge. Finally, as the authors explore the historical-philosophical nature of our disciplines, it turns out it is precisely this sense of imagination that not only blurs the lines—and broadens the scholarly possibilities—between history and philosophy but also the humanities and the sciences writ large, a matter taken up in the second half of this volume.

Bryan Warnick's chapter, "Why Does History Matter to Philosophy?," introduces us to the recurring theme of the unexamined, occult aspects of the human experiences that lie beyond our own and how we are often "blind to the meanings that people attach to objects and events around them." Warnick invokes William James's belief that "overcoming this blindness is precisely the job of education" because it expands our ability to see the world as others see it. Warnick proposes that this is also the purpose of philosophy: to push "against the invincible blindness to more fully recognize the infinite range of possible meaning lying around us."

History, he argues, is crucial to overcoming James's notion of blindness because history provides the context for what is meaningful to us. Indeed, rather than envisioning philosophy as a rational activity, Warnick reminds us that major philosophers thought that "philosophy was motivated by deep emotions" (Warnick, chapter 1). History, in this sense, is a kind of daimon to philosophy, the spark behind a philosopher's intuitions about educational aims and values.

The nature of that spark is further elaborated in Bruce Kimball's chapter, where he traces the intuitive and imaginative dimensions of induction in historical reasoning. In his chapter on "Philosophy, Literature, and Inductive Historiography," Kimball problematizes commonly held beliefs about the inductive (and "putatively atheoretical nature") of historical method by elaborating five historically and philosophically significant perspectives on induction and comparing the nuanced accounts presented therein with the taken-for-granted assumptions regarding induction in most philosophical critiques of historical method.

Kimball argues that most critiques of the "putative weakness of historical reasoning" (Kimball, chapter 2) are based on enumerative induction notions that overlook the complicated nature and evolution of discussions concerning induction since the nineteenth century. Instead, Kimball argues most historical reasoning is based upon intuitive or imaginative inductive generalizations. Moreover, similar to induction in scientific discoveries, intuitive and imaginative induction in historical reasoning involves a "mysterious step" by which we pass from particulars to generals. Whereas Warnick argues for the value of historical intuitions to philosophical reasoning, Kimball argues there is something intuitive in the particulars to which historians attribute historical (general) significance.

Kimball's account of the nuanced types of induction that inform historical reasoning and their relationship to philosophy and literature suggests some of the blindness we have as philosophers and historians to each other's disciplinary practices. In so doing, he challenges conventional beliefs regarding what distinguishes philosophy, history, literature, and the social and natural sciences, a discussion taken up again by Samuel Rocha and Patti Lather in the final two chapters of this volume.

Jackie Blount's historical account of "The Mutual Intellectual Relationship of John Dewey and Ella Flagg Young: *Contributions to Education* Series, 1901–1902" demonstrates the blindness that can affect our understanding of influential educational thinkers when we have limited knowledge of the historical contexts and actors that influenced their thought and work. Blount's study of Ella Flagg Young's contributions as an educator and scholar recovers an important figure that has gone largely forgotten in the history of education. Her disappearance—including her self-imposed desire to leave few traces of her personal life—resonates with the importance given to uncovering historical actors and philosophers rendered silent or invisible in our prevailing disciplinary narratives in Antoinette Errante's chapter.

But beyond "recovering" Ella Flagg Young, Blount's work challenges prevailing beliefs concerning the provenance of John Dewey's educational thought. Through Blount's analysis of their mutual intellectual engagement, we learn of the woman whose experience as an educator and administrator became the spark igniting Dewey's sudden interest in education in the years in which their collaboration flourished.

The broadened intellectual visions made possible through cross-disciplinary work is taken up by Joe Watras in his chapter, "Blending the Philosophy and the History of Education: Discussion of the Works of Boyd Bode, Bernard Mehl, and Maxine Greene." Watras reminds us of the historical context giving rise to the history and philosophy of education: the establishment of the Social Foundations of Education in the early part of the twentieth century and its mission to help "educators develop interpretive, normative, and critical perspectives about education" (Watras, chapter 4).

Watras demonstrates how disciplines outside of our own can spark our scholarship through the example of logician Boyed Bode's philosophical engagement with (and critique of) the psychologists and curriculum theorists enamored with the scientific progressive movement of the first half of the nineteenth century, Bernard Mehl's use of history to explore persistence and change in the philosophical orientations of American education, and Maxine Greene's use of literature as foil to philosophical and historical narratives of education. Watras's exploration of these three scholars' studies not only reveals the complementary ways in which historical and philosophical accounts can identify persistence and change in our values, attitudes, behaviors, and beliefs concerning education but also the value of other disciplinary traditions—such as literature—as sparks and alternative lenses through which to understand educational problems and processes.

In their chapters, historian Ben Johnson and philosopher Tom Falk utilize very different historico-philosophical approaches to explore the ways in which our taken for granted beliefs and assumptions about education are embedded in contemporary ideological beliefs that can influence our historical reasoning of the past as well as our current understanding of what constitutes the past.

In his chapter, "A Historical Analysis of 'Free Money Ideology' and Ohio State University President George W. Rightmire, 1926–1938," for instance, Ben Johnson brings together an analysis of an emerging ideology regarding university fundraising and a historical case study. Johnson argues that it would be difficult to understand the meaning behind Rightmire's strategies unless we took into account that the idea of "free money"—the practice of raising unencumbered endowment funds, a financial strategy that we have come to take for granted in higher education—was just beginning to emerge during this period. While Blount's chapter shows the importance of understanding the historical context influencing philosophers and their ideas, Johnson emphasizes the importance of understanding extant and emerging values and beliefs in order to assign meaning to historical actors.

Tom Falk's chapter, "History as Critique and Source of Ideology in Education: Tucson's Outlawed Mexican American Studies Program," on the other hand, is a philosophical meditation on the ideological nature of history itself. While historians are unlikely to quibble with Falk's argument that history textbooks always represent a selective—and therefore inherently ideological—tradition, his critique of Tucson's outlawed Mexican American Studies Program (MASP) reminds us that we should be wary even of revisionist attempts to redress those aspects of the past that have been written out. Falk troubles the MASP curriculum's attempt to recover a Mesoamerican past by pointing to the numerous nonliterate indigenous traditions, which Falk refers to as "the people without history," that the MASP counter-narrative leaves out. Falk then asks us to imagine what it might be like to envision history education in ways he argues are representative of these nonliterate indigenous societies and therefore beyond ideology. It is a philosopher's invitation to use our imagination of peoples often disappeared in our narratives to rethink history and historical reasoning.

Falk's invitation to imagine alternative possibilities is a fitting way to end the first part of the book and introduce the second part of the book, where authors attend more specifically to the matter of how related studies of philosophy and history contribute to knowledge and research about education. A central significant claim found across the chapters is that related studies of philosophy and history of education can entertain possibilities and insights into educational studies that are greater than those either discipline can accomplish on its own. They demonstrate this by providing examples of how related historical and philosophical work can contribute to educational policy, teaching practice and research, sensibilities regarding historical actors and philosophers rendered invisible in our prevailing disciplinary discourses, and our understanding of the possibilities presented by the increasingly blurred lines between and among the humanities and the social and natural sciences.

In their chapter that opens the second half of the book, "A Modest Plea for Collaborative History and Philosophy of Education," philosopher Randall Curren and historian Charles Dorn share the process by which they worked on a study of patriotism in schools for a book series for which Curren is coeditor with Jonathan Zimmerman. The story of their sustained collaboration documents the unexpected developments that occurred when they began to share their separate philosophical and historical drafts and realized that they would need to address and somehow close the conceptual distances resulting from their separate disciplinary perspectives.

Over the course of sustained dialogue and collaborative writing, they demonstrate how they were able to weave together "the threads of historical and philosophical inquiry onto the fabric of a more coherent interpretation" (Curren and Dorn, chapter 7) that provided a more nuanced guide for parents and administrators regarding the relationship between civic and patriotic education than either could have written on their own. Moreover, their experience demonstrates why, for many complex educational problems and questions, related philosophical and historical work benefits from sustained transdisciplinary collaborations rather than interdisciplinary work.

While Curren and Dorn suggest how collaborative historical and philosophical work can inform contemporary educational policy and curriculum studies, Winston C. Thompson addresses the value of related philosophical and historical work for teaching practice and research in his chapter, "Educational Practice in Pursuit of Justice Requires Historically Informed and Philosophically Rigorous Scholarship." Thompson argues that in order for liberal educators to attain justice aims in their teaching, their decision-making requires "historical sensitivity and normative conceptual clarity" (Thompson, chapter 8).

Thompson elaborates his argument by inviting the reader to imagine that a liberal educator is transported to an unknown world where her first task as a liberal educator is to attend to the realities of "quace," a characteristic of all individuals in this imagined society. By creating a hypothetical scenario about a social category to which we are "history blind," Thompson makes a compelling case for why the meaning of any social category cannot be fully grasped without a sense of the historical patterns of difference in which they are embedded and how these patterns over time are understood through normative philosophical dimensions of liberal progress and justice. If philosophy provides the educator with the tools through which to understand the aims and values of education and its relationship to quace (or any social category), history provides a lens through which to understand the ways in which quace constructed difference and, likely, different ontological realities for individuals in our hypothetical society.

Antoinette Errante also explores the value of transdisciplinary engagement for the purposes of developing historical sensitivity and normative conceptual clarity but with respect to the ways in which collaborative work can make our disciplinary tents more inclusive. In her chapter, "The Predicament of Culture and Educational History and Philosophy as Reconciliation: Seeking out the 'Disappeared' through Transdisciplinary Engagement," Errante explores how the historical evolution of what constitutes "good philosophy" and "good history" has tended to universalize Western scholarly practices.

She suggests how philosophizing history and historicizing philosophy with culture in mind can help us deconstruct our unexamined assumptions about the universal nature of those practices and in so doing recover the historical actors and philosophers that we subsequently disappeared or rendered invisible. This entails an opening up of our disciplinary borders to new scholarly perspectives and sustained transdisciplinary engagement and dialogue that will likely challenge prevailing perspectives regarding what constitutes history and philosophy and who we think of as historical agents and thinkers of thoughts. Errante likens this process to the truth-telling and reconciliation processes that have been used to dismantle regimes of silence. She proposes that we build on Maria Lugones's (2006) concept of "complex communication."

While Lugones largely speaks about the communicative strategies that different marginalized groups might use to speak to each other, Errante suggests how Lugones's work can help us envision transdisciplinary dialogue that contributes to what Yancy (2015) refers to as "white double consciousness" so that we can overcome the blindness of our prevailing disciplinary practices and broaden our historical and philosophical understanding of the human experience.

The final three chapters address the value of transdisciplinary historical and philosophical work in relation to the social and natural sciences. If Kimball argues that it is not the imaginative spark that distinguishes history from philosophy, literature, or even science, the final chapters show us some of the kinds of productive turns knowledge can take if we consider the humanistic elements of our work as a spark that joins us to the natural and social sciences rather than as a characteristic that marginalizes us from them.

In their chapter, "James Bryant Conant, Science, and Science Education: The Uses of History and Philosophy," Wayne Urban and Sarah Wever explore the contributions of Conant's historical understanding of science and scientific discoveries to contemporary philosophy of science. At a time when faith in science's objectivity was hardly questioned, Conant interjected his philosophical and historically grounded understanding of the scientific method and the importance of imagination, serendipity, and dumb luck to scientific discovery. One has to wonder if Thomas Kuhn, Conant's teaching assistant, would have revolutionized our modern understanding of science had he not met and studied with Conant.

Kuhn is once again invoked as the beginning of the historical evolution of "social science wrestling with itself" (Lather, chapter 12) through which Patti Lather challenges Sam Rocha's proposal that we think of historical and philosophical educational approaches to method as "pre-qualitative." Rocha laments the precarious place on the academic totem pole those of us who labor in the humanities find ourselves within colleges of education, where we are rendered largely invisible next to the behemoth methodological complex that is quantitative and qualitative research.

Rocha argues the present state of affairs can be traced to Dewey's agenda for transforming education into a university discipline. While Dewey is considered a founding figure in the philosophy of education, Rocha argues that Dewey largely appealed to the scientific and psychological movements that dominated his times in order to make the case. He then proposes that we consider movements in post-qualitative research exemplified by the work of Elizabeth St. Pierre as a means through which to "correct the foundational missteps of Dewey's scientific agenda for education" and consider historical and philosophical methods as "pre-qualitative" (Rocha, chapter 11).

In "The Blurring and Entanglement of Philosophy and Science: A Response," her historical rebuttal to Rocha's chapter, Patti Lather suggests that Rocha, "conflates social science, scientism, and science itself, sometimes writ large and sometimes its variant." By characterizing philosophy and history as pre-qualitative, Lather argues that Rocha does not take into account the ways in which the social sciences and the sciences have been wrestling with philosophical and humanistic concerns ever since Kuhn revolutionized our understanding of scientific discoveries.

Lather reminds Rocha that the current state of educational research can hardly be laid at Dewey's doorstep since Dewey's vision ultimately lost the fight to Thorndike's psychometrics, a loss from which education has yet to recover. Rather than being pre-qualitative, Lather argues that St. Pierre is making a case for a return "to the entanglement of science and philosophy at its modern roots" (Lather, chapter 12). The result has been an increasing blurring between the humanities, the social sciences, and even the sciences over the last forty years, efforts that can be seen, for example, in educational philosophers' attempts to wrest testing away from the neoliberal framework of value.

The exchange between Rocha and Lather reminds us just how productive transdisciplinary dialogue can be in helping us overcome the blindnesses of our disciplines. We are all sparked by our natural inclinations to see and ask questions about the human experience through certain disciplinary lenses, but we hope that with this volume we convey the value of working across disciplines and on the margins of dissent, confusion, and the established conventional visions of our disciplines. We look forward to more colleagues joining us in this conversation.

I

The Relationship between Philosophical and Historical Study of Education

Chapter One

Why Does History Matter to Philosophy?

Bryan R. Warnick

After my first semester of college, I lived for two years in Buenos Aires, Argentina. Every day, I would walk the busy and vibrant streets of "La Capital Federal," as the locals call it. I ate mountains of grilled meat, drank *máte*, learned Spanish (much of it now forgotten), and developed an interest in international *fútbol*. The major streets—streets like *Corrientes*, *Avenida 9 de Julio*, and *Sarmiento*—became well known and familiar to me, as did the peculiarities of *los porteños*, the citizens of Buenos Aires, with their distinct mix of warmth and almost theatrical bravado.

It was one of the formative experiences of my life. I enjoyed most of the positive aspects of Argentine culture. And yet, once in a while, I sensed an ocean of dark memories lying just below the pavement of the famous streets. I would hear hushed talk of *Las Malvinas*, the Falkland Islands. I would catch a dark glance as conversation turned to politics. I would read revolutionary graffiti, often extolling the virtues of *El Che*, the famous Argentine revolutionary Ernesto "Che" Guevara.

None of this should have been at all surprising. After all, I was there only twenty years after the massacre near the Ezeiza airport, the final curtain call for the dashed hopes of Peronism. I was there only seventeen years after the *Madres de la Plaza de Mayo*, the Mothers of the Disappeared, began protesting the loss of their missing children on the steps of the presidential palace. I was there just eleven years after the humiliating war for the Falklands. I was there just ten years after the removal of the military dictatorship that had waged a brutal "dirty war" against left-wing political dissidents, including taking some of them on notorious *vuelos de la muerte* (death flights) where perceived political opponents of the military junta would be drugged, stripped, and tossed from airplanes into the Atlantic. I was there just five years after hyperinflation had devastated the economy. While I was there, the AMIA Jewish community center was bombed, killing eighty-five people, not far away from where I was living, an incident that has never been explained. The darkness in 1994, when I arrived there, was not even a distant memory but a cloud still hanging low over the city, mingling with the smog.

As I walked the streets of Buenos Aires, I was vaguely aware of some of this, but mostly I was just ignorant and blind. None of this was present to me as I enjoyed *asado* and watched the tango. As I navigated the landscape of this vibrant and complex city, I was insensitive to its darkest nooks and crannies, to the sadness and sense of loss around every corner, the skeletons in the closets.

As an example of my blissful stupefaction, I would sometimes pass by a handsome, colonnaded set of buildings known as *la Escuela Superior de Mecánica de la Armada* (the Navel Mechanics School). At that time, I did not know that this was a site where thousands of political prisoners were tortured, electrocuted on steel beds in tiny cells. I did not know that babies born there were stripped from their mothers and distributed to families of the military junta, did not know that of the 5,000 prisoners once held there only 150 lived to talk about it (Daniels 2008), and did not know that this building would one day be the national museum of human rights. None of this was present in my mind at the time; it was just another European-style building, quite common in Buenos Aires. I am now amazed, and a bit ashamed, at how little I grasped of the meanings behind the landscape passing around me. Because I was ignorant, I didn't *care* about where I was in the way that I should have cared.

As I think about my situation in this city, I think of the essay by William James, "On a Certain Blindness in Human Beings." In the essay, James argues that we are blind to the meanings that people attach to objects and events around them. This blindness occurs, James writes, because "our judgments concerning the worth of things, big or little, depend on the feelings the things arouse in us" (James 1902, 229). What we care about in life is a product of past associations between ideas, things, people, and events, and this is all very personal. Our emotional lives, moreover, are tied to our practical lives. Past associations are what motivate our current actions. The key emotions in our active lives are, first, eagerness ("wherever a process of life communicates an eagerness to him who lives it," James writes, "there the life becomes genuinely significant" [234]) and, second, joy ("to miss the joy is to miss all" [240]).

Other people often lack the emotional connections that we have to our own practical tasks. They lack our eagerness and our joy, and they cannot understand why we do what we do. They cannot understand why we care about football games on Saturdays or why we spend so much money and time on seemingly trivial hobbies. One of my personal passions, for example, is amateur astronomy. I particularly enjoy looking at deep-sky objects, such as galaxies and nebulae. Through my little telescope, though, these objects are quite unimpressive—dim smudges of light, really. Being able to locate and view such objects is thrilling to me, and yet other people often can't understand why. As James would say, we are all blind to the "vital secrets" in each other's lives (230)—"vital" both in the sense of being absolutely necessary and of being full of driving energy—"hence," James writes, "the stupidity and injustice of our opinions, so far as they deal with the significance of alien lives" (230). We can't see what is most important to others: "Our private power of sympathetic vibration with other lives," James bemoans, "gives out so soon" (James 1960, 173).

James says that overcoming this blindness, at least to some extent, is precisely the job of education. He writes, "Education, enlarging as it does our horizon and perspective, is a means of multiplying our ideals, of bringing new ones into view" (James 1902, 293). In other words, education is about grasping the deeper meanings behind why people enjoy what they do. What do people see in Picasso? What do they hear in Mozart? How does it feel to solve a math problem or write a poem? Education is about shifting our attention, noticing what was hidden in the lives of others, breaking the habitual focus of consciousness to include a wider scope of reality moving around us. Through education, we increase that "sympathetic vibration" to more and more of what lies around us. Being educated to overcome blindness, it could even be said, is developing the "faculty of perceiving in an unhabitual way" (James 2007, 110), the faculty that James says is the essence of genius. The more we understand the many ways people find meaning and significance in the world, the more we break from our dusty and tired habits of thought.

For my purposes here, it is important to point out that we could probably say that same thing about philosophy. Philosophy, like education, is about growth of understanding, about seeing new connections that were previously hidden. Philosophy, like education, is about pushing against the invincible blindness to more fully recognize the infinite range of possible meaning lying around us.

Now, I want to say that I experienced blindness in my engagement with the city of Buenos Aires. I missed the emotional core of the city, even though I lived and worked there for two years. Contrary to James, it wasn't that I had missed the hidden joy—in fact, I came to appreciate many of the beautiful things about Argentine culture that I was blind to before (Americans who try *máte* tell me that it tastes like drinking from a lawn mower, yet to me the taste is full of memory and emotion). Still, I had missed something important: I had missed the sorrow. I had not missed the eagerness; I had missed the hesitation. I had not missed the strenuous mood; I had missed the fear and dread. I had not missed the passionate intensity; I had missed the reluctance and insecurity. I was unable to fully experience the city that I thought I knew well, with its shadows and with its darkness. This handicapped my thinking, and I continued to perceive things in a habitual way.

What was I lacking during this time? What would have been the key to enriching my thinking? I think what allows us to experience something more fully, what allows us to overcome blindness and to see the meaningful connections in the world, is in large part a consciousness of history. James himself mentioned that personal meaning is built largely of historical associations, as individual emotions connect to activities and events. I think this also holds true on the level of community. The meaning of the colonnaded building for the community depended on historical associations, and these associations can be investigated through historical methods.

History, then, is what helps us to overcome Jamesean blindness. I believe that overcoming blindness is an essential step to knowing the world around us. Without history, we see the world as children. As Cicero said, "Not to know what happened before you were born is to be a child forever" (quoted in Jones 1969, 3). Consider one way in which overcoming blindness is essential to mature knowing: it allows us to be moved emotionally, and being moved is an important part of inquiry. Sometimes, we think of philosophy as a purely rational activity, an abstract mind executing logic. But many major philosophers, such as Plato and Dewey, thought that philosophy was motivated by deep emotions, such as *eros*, a desire or love of something beyond oneself. Plato suggested that Socrates's inquiry was guided by a *daimon*, a being halfway between a god and a human being. A daimon served as an intermediary between desire and the object of longing. It was a type of inner voice, urging Socrates toward wisdom. It is not wrong to consider history to be a type of daimon to philosophy, an intermediary that pushes along inquiry. It is a voice that moves us with powerful emotions to investigate, to begin the journey out of the cave and up the ladder, toward greater understanding. Had I known about the Naval Mechanics School, I would have almost certainly been curious and called by the voice of history to find out more. I imagine I would have been "moved" to venture inside and to contribute to furthering the memory of the place. The echoes of pain emanating from the walls would have touched me deeply. I would have wanted to know more.

Now, here is the point of my extended analogy as it relates to philosophy of education and my diversion in William James. I think many of us, philosophers and lay commentators alike, are like my younger self bumbling around the city of Buenos Aires when we try to understand schools and education. Because we don't know the history, we cannot fathom the meaning. We miss the secret joy, and we miss the hidden sorrow. We miss it all. Many familiar practices in school take on a new significance when viewed in their historical context. For example, consider that extracurricular activities, I am told, were constructed as an attempt to create common experiences among students in the new comprehensive high schools. These schools had divided students into tracks, as was advocated by the administrative progressivism of the early twentieth century. In a sense, extracurricular activities are vestiges of a lost dream, a last nod to the common school, a last attempt to bring students from different classes and social backgrounds together in the democratic laboratories of schools. It is ironic that extracurricular activities are now seen mostly as developing a student's resume so he or she can better compete in the rat race of elite college admissions. They are about social division rather than democratic commonality.

How far reaching does this blindness corrupt the philosophical enterprise? To answer this question, we might turn to someone who is not a philosopher or a historian, George S. Counts, a well-known twentieth-century sociologist, educational thinker, and activist. Lost among his other provocative writings is a little article he originally published in 1929, "Criteria for Judging a Philosophy of Education." In this article, Counts lists a number of criteria useful in evaluating educational ideas. Counts's first criterion is that the philosophy must be empirically sound. By this, he means that a philosophy of education should be consistent with experience or, more bluntly, get the facts right. Counts points to scientific truths as one of the most important realms of facts. He calls science "that most refined body of human experience" ([1929] 1969, 92). He also makes room for metaphysical truths, ethical truths, and aesthetic truths. A philosophy of education must be consistent with these realms of human experience. It is notable, I think, that Counts does not single out history as a realm of human experience important to judging a philosophy of education. We can and should add it to the list. However, we could also point out that *all* empirical knowledge is, to some extent, historical knowledge. It is not just one discipline alongside others. What we know of science is really just a report on the history of scientific investigation. So history should have a special place among Counts's sources of experience. It is the collection of human experience.

The second criterion for evaluating a philosophy of education is that a philosophy of education needs to be "consistent in its several departments" (91). One cannot advocate for democratic ideals in theory and then act like a totalitarian in practice without at least a *prima facie* contradiction. The third criterion is that a philosophy of education should be "comprehensive" (93). This means that a philosophy of education should not leave out important aspects of the educational process. It should address the goals of education and also the pedagogies and institutions that will be necessary to achieve those goals. The fourth criterion is that a philosophy of education should be "practicable in its provisions" (93). This means that a philosophy of education should be realistic. It cannot be a set of pie-in-the-sky ideas, great in theory but impossible to execute in everyday life. Fifth, philosophy of education should be "satisfactory of its adherents" (94). I do not know exactly what

Counts meant by this, but I think he was saying that philosophy should be presented in a way that can move people to action (here again we see the importance of "being moved" in philosophy). It is a rhetorical point.

Now, I think that our knowledge of history is related to each of these other criteria, in addition to the criterion of empirical correctness that I just discussed. That is, the level of our historical consciousness will determine, in part, how well we are able to utilize each of these remaining four criteria. Think of the criterion of being "comprehensive" and being "consistent." It may seem at first that these are questions that can be answered in a fluffy philosophical armchair. It is clear, however, that certain inconsistencies are sometimes only apparent looking backward. That is, a practice may not seem incompatible with democratic ideals until we see how it has played out in the past. It may be that a school-choice scheme may be very democratic in theory but in practice be hijacked by corporate interests or other nondemocratic forces. Similarly, we might only know what we have left out of our theory when a gaping hole is exposed as an idea is implemented through time. The same holds true as we think about the criterion of being practicable. Again, it seems we do not know how well something might work until we have actually tried it in practice, and history is in a sense a record of our educational practices, successes, and failures. What about the criterion of being satisfactory to its adherents? On this point, it seem unlikely one would know how to "move" people, or argue effectively, until one knows the audience's history. To connect with an audience, one needs to know about their past. So, as we try to implement Counts's five criteria for evaluating a philosophy of education, we see that wisdom comes only after time has passed, as we reflect on the day at its end.

Now, to finalize, let me turn away from the question of why history matters to philosophy and say something about *how* history informs philosophy. If you will indulge me, I might even narrow the question to be: "How does history inform *my* thinking about philosophy of education?"

I would note, first, that there is no easy way to explain the relationship between my philosophical thinking and my historical reading. If someone asked me to explain what historical ideas, events, or people have influenced my philosophy, I would have to think about it. I could eventually supply an answer: my work on student rights, for example, is littered with reflections on past events and cases. But I would say that my philosophy is not informed by simply applying the "conclusions of history" to a particular contemporary problem. Consider what we might call the "ethico-historical deduction" in education:

1. We have a contemporary problem.
2. Policy X worked (or did not work) in the past.
3. Therefore, we should (or should not) implement X.

As an example, consider the idea of racial integration:

1. We have a problem with racially segregated schools.
2. History shows that busing did not work in the past.
3. Therefore, busing should not be used in the future.

A moment's reflection reveals obvious problems with this ethico-historical deduction. We might ask, under what conditions can we say that a policy that did or did not work in the past would or would not work in the future? Was the failure of busing a problem with the busing policy itself or with some sort of historically contingent circumstance or flaw of implementation? This is similar to what has been called the "Quine-Duhem thesis" in the philosophy of science. According to that thesis, we can never logically tell if the results of a scientific experiment are due to the factors we are testing or due to a flawed assumption that we make about the surrounding conditions. For example, is an unexpected test result due to a flaw in a theory, or is it produced by faulty equipment, a sleepy research assistant making a mistake, or some other of the possibly infinite outside factors? So, for me at least, we do not justify educational practices by simply applying the "truths of history" to contemporary problems.

So, if not through ethico-historical deductions, how *does* history seem to enter my thinking? Rather than being able to recall the intricacies of how schools developed, and drawing from them deductions about educational practice, I think reading history simply gives philosophers a sense of how the world tends to work and how it tends not to work (I'm channeling somebody here, but I don't remember whom). Reading history builds intuitions. One intuition I have, for example, is that people who have advantages rarely give them up willingly, even in the face of compelling moral reasons. This is particularly true when it comes to giving up the advantages that people have in educating their children. Now, if pressed, I could probably give you some historical examples of this, but I could not tell you where I first learned it or even if it is logically justified based on all existing historical evidence. But I would bet that this intuition is not that far off, even if I could not justify its epistemic status. This historical "truth" has mostly entered my consciousness as something of a background intuition.

This intuition has greatly informed my thinking about the best ways to press for equality in educational opportunity. In the *Journal of Applied Philosophy*, I argued for a model of educational distribution that I based on a "modified threshold": all students are educated up to an Amy Gutmann–like democratic threshold, with an equalized distribution of state-provided educational resources after the threshold has been met—the last part stipulating what happens after the threshold is the "modification" (Warnick 2015). As is well known in educational ethics, a threshold approach leaves intact many educational advantages that the wealthy might have, even with the modification of equal distribution of public resources after the threshold is met. Instead of arguing for a stricter notion of equality, I argue for what I call an "external proviso." According to this proviso, the remaining inequalities in how children are educated should be accounted for outside of educational institutions through broader redistributive practices rather than trying to equalize educational opportunities in schools themselves. If we can equalize educational achievement, we can make inequality matter less in the distribution of social goods.

Why did I argue for this approach rather than a stricter notion of educational equality? Part of it was a moral principle that parents need to be given some freedom to educate their children as they see fit and that too stringent attempts to regulate educational distribution would intrude negatively into family life (for example, mandating the reading of bedtime stories). But there is also a concession to my historical intuitions of what is possible. My intuition is that intervening too much with educational distribution by basing it on pure moral principles will likely come with nasty side effects, as people resist curtailing the educational advantage they can give to their children. I never make that argument explicit, and I never justify it through historical argument. Yet that intuition is behind the scheme that I proposed. Some fights for social justice, I conclude with this intuition, should occur in other arenas.

I think it is very important, then, for philosophers to have a set of more or less justified intuitions about the way the world works. Any good student of philosophy needs also to be a student of history, which will help ensure these intuitions are more or less justified. And, every once in a while, it is important for philosophers to go back to try to make the historical assumptions explicit and see if the assumptions hold up to critical scrutiny.

The last thing to point out with respect to developing these intuitions is that general reading in history is just as important as reading in the history of schooling or formal education. Indeed, reading only in the history of education might give only a partial perspective on "how the world works." Obviously, history of schooling is essential in forming justified intuitions for philosophers of education, but it is not the only reading that should occur. Reading about the history of nations and peoples, of emperors and commoners, of wars and industries, of sports and sciences, of social movements, is also critical. This is, obviously, the work of a lifetime.

To summarize, then, history is essential to philosophy. It comes in the beginning of inquiry as history helps us to be moved by the world—moved to ask questions and pursue greater understanding. As we overcome our blindness, we have more opportunities to be touched emotionally by what surrounds us. It is a daimon that moves our inquiry forward. History should also be a part of how we formulate our own ideas, not in the sense of making deductions based on historical truths but by being guided by intuitions of how the world works. These intuitions are shaped by broad and deep readings of not only the history of education but also of the history of humanity broadly conceived. Finally, history aids philosophy at the end of inquiry as we evaluate a philosophy of education once it is developed. It helps us to do the things George Counts suggested as we evaluate educational ideas. In short, as we engage with history, we can walk those streets of Buenos Aires not as children but as mature beings sensitive to the light and darkness, the joy and the sorrow, desiring to understand.

REFERENCES

Counts, George. (1929) 1969. "Criteria for Judging a Philosophy of Education." In *What Is Philosophy of Education?*, edited by C. Lucas, 90–94. New York: Macmillan.
Daniels, Alfonso. 2008. "Argentina's Dirty War: The Museum of Horrors." *Telegraph*, May 17. http://www.telegraph.co.uk/culture/3673470/Argentinas-dirty-war-the-museum-of-horrors.html.
James, William. 1902. *Talks to Teachers on Psychology: And to Students on Some of Life's Ideals*. Cambridge, MA: Holt.
———. 1960. *The Will to Believe, Human Immortality, and Other Essays in Popular Philosophy*. Mineola, NY: Dover.
———. 2007. *The Principles of Psychology*. Vol. 2. New York: Cosimo Classics.
Jones, Tom Bard. 1969. *From the Tigris to the Tiber: An Introduction to Ancient History*. Madison, WI: Dorsey.
Warnick, Bryan R. 2015. "Taming the Conflict over Educational Equality." *Journal of Applied Philosophy* 32:50–66.

Chapter Two

Philosophy, Literature, and Inductive Historiography

Bruce A. Kimball

The complex relationship between philosophy and history becomes especially significant in colleges and schools of education. While philosophers and historians need not interact in other faculties, the predominance of non-humanistic culture in the field of education forces philosophers and historians to become allies and friends. However, when attempting to collaborate in scholarship, philosophers and historians of education often discover that their friends seem more like the enemies of their enemies. Their work and methods may appear incompatible, even incomprehensible to the other.

The differences are expressed in their parodies of each other's work. Often historical colleagues announce that philosophers "just make it up." Without gathering and sifting the evidence, philosophers posit a "likely" or a "let us suppose," and then they are off inferring and rebutting without looking back, leaving historians muttering about sources and evidence. Conversely, as philosopher Phil Smith has often said, "historians just tell stories." There is scarcely any theory or deep argument in historiography. The philosophical critique of historiography as storytelling complements the widely held view that historiography is "literature"—subjective, invented, and relativistic. By either account, historiographical reasoning is weak, if it exists at all, and historiography contributes little to knowledge, aside from compiling facts.

It is often observed that historical scholarship is inductive in the general sense that historians attend to evidence. But this observation points to the deeper truth that historians find meaning in the particular. Principles, rules, standards, and concepts—particularly about the past—acquire their meaning only in particular instances in original sources. And this meaning almost always turns out to be complicated, belying the abstractions. Taking these points for granted, this chapter examines at a very practical level the inductive reasoning of historians working in original research. As a prelude to that endeavor, this chapter considers the relationship of historiographical reasoning to philosophy, on the one hand, and to literature, on the other.

PHILOSOPHY AND LITERATURE

One definition of "philosophy," as it is practiced by philosophers, is necessarily brief and simple. First, philosophy is a method, not a system of thought or doctrine. Second, that method addresses the reasoning in argumentation. Philosophers analyze and synthesize reasoned arguments, drawing from their "toolbox," as Randy Curren mentions in this volume. Lastly, philosophy examines and evaluates deductive reasoning, in particular. Philosophers assess the validity of the complex chain of syllogisms in arguments on virtually any subject.

One subject that philosophers have addressed incisively is the nature of inductive arguments. Their deductive reasoning has contributed greatly to understanding induction, which is the reasoning between particulars and generalizations. The distinction between these two kinds of logic requires some explanation.

Aristotle first explained the syllogism, and he was therefore extolled in the medieval universities that effectively viewed deduction as scientific method. When the revolution in natural sciences commenced in the seventeenth century, the English philosopher Francis Bacon redefined scientific method to mean inductive inference from empirical evidence. During the first half of the nineteenth century in the United States, philosophers and scientists followed Bacon by enshrining induction and anathematizing Aristotle (Daniels 1968; Bozeman 1977; Urbach 1987).

During this "Baconian Age," two significant confusions arose concerning induction. Some scientists and philosophers conflated it with empiricism by failing to distinguish between examining evidence and reasoning between particulars and generalizations. For example, measuring the air temperature at 7 a.m., noon, and 7 p.m. is one thing. Inferring a general conclusion from these three measurements is another. The latter is one form of induction. This distinction is important in appreciating historiography because historical evidence is often difficult to find and examine. The empirical difficulties of historians can contribute to their reasoning appearing simple or suspect.

A second confusion arose because most philosophers and scientists treated induction and deduction as converse forms of reasoning. "In Deduction we infer particular from general truths; while in Induction we infer general from particular," writes William Whewell in the 1840s, as does John Stuart

Mill (Whewell quoted in Copi 1972, 24; see Mill 1874, 153–54). This view predominated among scientists through the beginning of the twentieth century and persisted much later in discussion of historiography (Fischer 1970).

In certain forms, deduction and induction do seem to operate conversely. For example, from the three air-temperature measurements at 7 a.m., noon, and 7 p.m., one might inductively infer that mornings and evenings are cooler than noontime. Compare that reasoning to the classical deductive syllogism: All women are mortal. Sappho is a woman. Therefore, Sappho is mortal.

At first glance, it seems that we reasoned from particular temperatures to the generalization via induction and from all women to the particular case of Sappho via deduction. But deduction concerns the relationship among sets, and in this example, Sappho constitutes a set with one member. Hence, induction is not the converse of deduction, as Morris Cohen and Ernest Nagel note in 1934 (273–76). Induction is a different kind of reasoning. If so, then how is this historiographical reasoning related to literature?

In 1973, the medieval historian Hayden White published *Metahistory: The Historical Imagination in Nineteenth-Century Europe*. This book intended to explain the nature and method of historiography by examining eight major European historians and philosophers of history from the early nineteenth century. White adopts this indirect approach because these eight "master" scholars considered "historical knowledge" to be "an autonomous domain in the spectrum of the human and physical sciences" with "unique characteristics of a specifically *historical method* of inquiry" (1973, 1).

By 1970, however, two groups had presented serious challenges to the epistemic foundation of historical scholarship, White observes. On the one hand, a number of critical theorists on the European Continent had "cast serious doubts on the value of . . . historical reconstructions, and challenged history's claims to a place among the sciences" (White 1973, 1–2). On the other hand, Anglo-American analytic philosophers had questioned the "epistemological status and cultural function of historical thinking" and raised "doubts about history's status as either a rigorous science or a genuine art" (2). This two-pronged critique led to viewing "historical consciousness as a specifically Western prejudice by which the presumed superiority of modern, industrial society can be retroactively substantiated" (2).

In response, White "intended to provide a new perspective on the current debate over the nature and function of historical knowledge" (2). His analysis became a landmark in the theory of historiography. "Study any textbook on the theory and philosophy of history, and you will be assured that his 1973 book *Metahistory* marked a revolutionary turning point in historical theory" (Timmins 2011, 1).

White begins by observing the paradox that "the histories produced by the master historians of the nineteenth century display radically different conceptions of . . . historical work" (1973, 4). From there, White sets forth his theory of the nature of historiography and historical method while drawing on literary scholars, including Northrup Frye and Kenneth Burke, and sociologists, particularly Karl Mannheim (White 1973). Observers also note similarities between White and his "contemporaries Thomas Kuhn and Michel Foucault" (Timmins 2011, 1).

White maintains that historians begin their work by identifying facts about a subject that they assemble into a "chronicle" (1973, 6). They then engage in "emplotment" by imposing a narrative structure on the chronicle while presupposing certain ideologies and forms of arguments (7). Specifically, historians employ four types of narrative, four kinds of argument, and four ideologies, as well as "four principal tropes of poetic language" (7–29, 31). White thus develops a formal historiographical schema to classify virtually any historical work (29).

White's schema entails these basic theses. First, historians do not "find" history; they imaginatively "invent" it. Thus, history is literature, and writing history is "an essentially poetic act" (White 1973, x, 6). Second, historical narrative is *a priori* and subjective. Historians presuppose kinds of arguments and ideologies and infuse their subjectivity in the narrative. Third, the process is inevitable. Historians cannot avoid imposing a narrative fraught with *a priori* argument and ideology.

The final thesis is relativism. White finds no basis for determining "whether a given historian's work is a better, or more correct, account of . . . the historical process than some other historian's account" (1973, 3). He subsequently declares, "There can be no such thing as a non-relativistic representation of historical reality" (Quoted in Paul 2011, 96; see Timmins 2011).

RESPONSES TO *METAHISTORY*

Metahistory rapidly became a singular authority in historiography, credited with initiating "the linguistic turn" or "narrative turn" in historical theory and writing (Timmins 2011, 1; Levisohn 2010, 4). In 2011, a biography of White was published, and one reviewer observes that *Metahistory* "has inspired legions of acolytes whose reverence for the master at times verges on embarrassing" (Timmins 2011, 1; see Paul 2011). But most of these acolytes professed outside history departments. Academic and professional historians generally gave *Metahistory* "a cool reception," and some have argued that White's "influence on the actual practice of history and historical writing has been virtually zero" (Timmins 2011, 1). In fact, his culminating academic appointment was in the comparative literature department, not the history department, at Stanford University.

In the view of some historians, White attacks a straw man. *Metahistory* assumes that early nineteenth-century European historians provided models of how historians think and work. But in the post-Euclidean world of the twentieth century, historians had already come to appreciate the interpretive and inventive character of their work. Other historians hold that White's assault on academic historiography exaggerates that interpretive and inventive character. If historians just impose narratives based on their own assumptions, then what happens in historical research? Do historians learn nothing by studying original sources, archives, statistics, and other data from the past?

The debate stimulated by White's "linguistic turn" came to focus on "the much vexed problems" of historical narrative (Cronon 1992, 1350). Where do historical narratives originate? How are they constructed? What is their validity? In subsequent writing, White maintains that the narratives "imposed" on the facts come from the "imagination" of historians (Levisohn 2010, 7). Given the imaginary origins of historical narratives, "the best grounds for choosing one perspective on history rather than another are ultimately aesthetical or moral rather than epistemological" (White 1973, xii).

Certain sympathetic critics subsequently try to refine White's account of historical narrative while also providing a basis for its epistemic validity. Invoking phenomenology, some maintain that historians, like other scholars, create narratives from the moment they encounter data about events (Carr 1986). By this view, historians do not proceed in steps through the imaginative imposition of narrative upon an event. Rather, "the event is narrativized from . . . the first experience of the event" (Levisohn 2010, 11). Adumbrating this phenomenological view, other scholars invoke anthropologists, such as Clifford Geertz, and argue that historians build their narratives from other narratives, including secondary literature, accounts of the general background, primary accounts from the participants in the historical event, and historians' own predispositions, assumptions, and concerns (Levisohn 2010, 12–15).

But these gambits do not explain, "How can we tell the difference between those narratives that are accurate and those that are not?" (Levisohn 2010, 11). Furthermore, despite his express relativism, White has a "positivist" view of facts and affirms that "the historian has a responsibility to get those facts right, on the basis of the best evidence available" (Kansteiner 1993, 274; see Levisohn 2010, 5; and see White 1973, 5–6). Therefore, he implies that facts are related to historical generalizations or narratives in some significant way.

However, White, his followers, and his critics did not analyze the kind of reasoning that relates general conclusions to particular facts ascertained from evidence. This is induction, the fundamental reasoning of historiography. To be sure, historians do other kinds of reasoning, such as hypothetico-deductive reasoning, in which a hypothesis is advanced, one or more implications are deduced, and then the historian looks for evidence to confirm or rebut the deductions, in order to confirm or rebut the initial hypothesis. Nevertheless, the characteristic reasoning in historiography is induction, which has been overlooked in discussions about historical method. Many historical articles and even books can be construed as extended efforts to gather and examine facts in relation to one general thesis or hypothesis.

INDUCTIVE REASONING

Study of induction in the United States commenced early in the 1800s and continued through the end of the 1900s, commensurate with the increasing emphasis given to natural science. In 1859, the publication of Charles Darwin's *Origin of Species* intensified that study because Darwin's inferences from the fossil record clearly involved induction (Ghiselin 1969). During the fifty years after the Civil War, the immense literature on induction grew larger, as the emerging social sciences tried to adopt the method of natural science (Bruce 1987; Ross 1991).

Through the 1910s, scientists and philosophers reached little consensus on the nature and operation of scientific method apart from agreeing that inductive reasoning played a central role. In the 1950s, induction was still considered "one of the most hotly debated issues of modern philosophy" and "the central issue in any philosophy of science" (Kemeny 1963, 711). Drawing on this literature, this chapter identifies five philosophically and historically prominent accounts of induction that inform our understanding of historiographical reasoning and its relation to philosophy and literature.

The first account is enumeration. According to *enumerative induction*, one examines every member of a set or class and then infers a general conclusion that describes the set. Francis Bacon was traditionally understood to conceive induction in this way (Urbach 1987; Vickers 1992). Suppose, for example, that Jackie Blount studied female school principals who worked in Chicago during the calendar year 1905 and she concluded that none of them had married. According to enumerative induction, Jackie would reach this conclusion by identifying and studying all such principals and then infer that all of them were single.

This additive account is reductionist, however, and does not comprehend many practical and conceptual problems of inductive research. What if the set is very large or the members are difficult to find or study? By the mid-nineteenth century, these problems led to rejecting enumeration as an adequate account of scientific induction, except for simple straightforward inquiries (Daniels 1968; Bruce 1987).

Likewise, practical and conceptual problems arising in detailed empirical research mean that enumerative induction rarely explains historians' reasoning. What if a female principal is secretly married or barred from marrying someone with whom she cohabits? How is she counted? Suppose the boundaries of the school district of Chicago are not congruent with the city or the boundaries of the district or the city have changed over time. Definitions of historical classes and members are often indefinite and variable, making it difficult or impossible to enumerate generalizations that can become premises of complex syllogistic reasoning.

A second account of induction is *verification*, which was identified by J. F. W. Herschel in 1830 (164). In verification, one begins with a generalization that fits some members of a certain class and then checks the generalization against other members of the class. According to this account, Jackie might have read that female principals did not marry, so she tested this generalization against each succeeding principal working in Chicago in 1905, whom she identified. This process would be inductive verification. While the result may be the same as in enumerative induction, the methods differ significantly.

Moving from all the particulars to the generalization, enumerative induction is retrospective, summative, and discrete and apparently yields certainty. Moving from generalization to successive particulars, inductive verification is iterative and provisional, because one is continually examining additional members of the class. In addition, the number and identity of all the members may not be clear. Scientists and philosophers through the twentieth century continued to credit Herschel's inductive verification, as did Thomas Kuhn in 1962 (8–9). But they have also recognized that this view is incomplete because verification does not explain the origin of generalizations.

In 1843, John Stuart Mill proposed a third view of induction that combined verification with an account of the formation of generalizations (1874, 330). Rejecting enumerative induction, Mill asserts that "all inference is from particulars to particulars" (1874, 146, 278–91, 393–97). Such inference has come to be called *analogical induction*, and Mill devised four rules of similarity and difference that govern reasoning "from particulars to particulars" and that still appear in logic textbooks today. Analogical induction generally adopts this form:

Lynda Stone and Winston Thompson are philosophers.
Lynda is brilliant.
Therefore, Winston is brilliant.

If we verified that Winston is brilliant, the next inductive inference would be to the generalization that "all philosophers are brilliant."

Jackie Blount's historical reasoning might be construed to follow Mill's account. Having identified and studied one female principal, Jackie examined and compared a second for differences and similarities. Noticing that neither was married, Jackie wondered if a third might be unmarried. Finding this to be true, Jackie thought, "Perhaps all female principals were unmarried" and then began employing inductive verification. Each time another female principal turned out to be unmarried, Jackie verified her generalization, while the probability increased that all female principals were unmarried. Understood in this way, historical research seems to fit analogical induction, which refutes enumerative induction and incorporates inductive verification.

Mill's account was regarded as the most compelling view of induction until the end of the nineteenth century. At that point, the consensus shifted as philosophers of science came to agree that analogical induction fits the analysis of particulars that have well-defined attributes known in advance but does not explain the discovery of generalizations.

Discovery is the fundamental issue, because induction is "ampliative," as Charles Peirce famously termed it (1931). A deductive syllogism does not increase knowledge because the conclusion is implied in the premises. But an induction amplifies knowledge by inferring a conclusion that goes beyond the premises. The inferences that "Winston is brilliant" and that "all philosophers are brilliant" are not implied within the premises above. The cost of the amplification, so to speak, is that the conclusions are provisional until we have examined all the evidence. Even then, analogical inferences are probable and always admit the possibility of being overturned in light of future evidence that contradicts the conclusion (Cohen 1989, 1). In contrast, a valid deductive syllogism establishes a necessary relationship between the premises and conclusion.

A fundamental issue for induction, then, is the discovery of an original generalization. Mill sidestepped this issue by contending that induction involves only two things: the *data* and the *method* of comparing similarity and difference (1874, 141–46, 291). His four rules do include a criterion of salience. For example, according to Mill, one knows that the induction above is more probable than this one:

Lynda Stone and Winston Thompson are philosophers.
Lynda is a vegetarian.
Therefore, Winston is a vegetarian.

But how does the mind determine that brilliance may be more salient to philosophy than is vegetarianism? Or that the length of a honeybee's proboscis is relevant to their survival in certain habitats, as Charles Darwin proposed?

These examples are not mysterious. But the question becomes profound when a radically new insight is involved. Mill does not address this question, and his contemporary, William Whewell ([1849] 1989), criticizes this oversight and proposes an alternative view. Virtually no one agreed with Whewell, except Charles Peirce, until the beginning of the twentieth century. At that point, philosophers of science began to endorse two explanations for the original discovery of an inductive generalization. These are the fourth and fifth accounts of induction.

The fourth may be called *type induction*, drawing upon the much debated idea of *epagoge* in Aristotle's *Posterior Analytics* (2002, II 19; see Milton 1987). *Epagoge* is commonly translated as "induction," and some philosophers in the twentieth century have termed it "intuitive" induction (Cohen and Nagel 1934, 275; Peters 1967, 58). But this rendering is somewhat misleading because *epagoge* refers to intellectual perception. Aristotle seems to say that, in examining a particular case, our minds can rationally perceive the attributes of the general set to which the case belongs.

The mind (*nous*) engages in a kind of "intellectual seeing" of the universal in one case, if we have the informed conceptual background to perceive it (Randall 1960, 44). For example, scientists needed only one skeleton in order to understand the nature of a *Tyrannosaurus rex*, given their prior knowledge of biology, dinosaurs, fossils, and so forth (Curren, e-mail message to author, January 26, 1993).

In 1912, John Dewey presents a similar conception in his essay "Induction and Deduction." Following Whewell and Peirce, Dewey criticizes Mill's view of analogical induction as "conventional and sterile." Dewey then argues that induction requires studying only "a typical case." He writes, "Induction consists in grasping what is *significant*, what is intellectually important, in any one [case]. . . . The trait of generalization found in induction does not primarily have to do with what is common to a number of cases. . . . Educationally, this means that it is important to deal with a *single* river basin as a typical case . . . rather than to deal superficially with a large number of river systems" (Dewey 1912, 424).

Type induction helps to explain certain kinds of historical research and reasoning. Consider Benjamin Johnson's dissertation, which examines the financial choices and failures of one major, midwestern, land-grant university in the 1920s and 1930s. Ben intends to publish a book that might be entitled: *Financial Struggles of the Midwestern, Land-Grant University in the 1920s and 1930s: Ohio State University*. Historians employ this format in titles all the time. What exactly do they mean?

Ben's argument would appear seriously deficient if conceived as enumerative induction, which requires examining every member of the class of institutions. Likewise, Ben's argument would appear weak if understood as analogical induction. The argument would need several more universities beyond the original case, because the research only becomes informative by identifying similarities and differences and verifying them with respect to successive particular cases. Under either account of induction, Ben's book would amount merely to "telling the story" of one university and lack "argument" or "theory" about the nature of these universities. Here is one of my central points. Charges about the putative weakness of historiographical reasoning rely on implicit definitions of inductive reasoning.

In contrast, Aristotle and Dewey suggest that examining more particular cases does not necessarily provide deeper understanding of the general type. Deep analysis of one case may be more informative. We do not know about the universities' finances, which is the particular subject of Ben's research. But we do know many attributes of the 1920s and 1930s and of major, midwestern, land-grant universities. Based on this conceptual background, perhaps Ben can perceive in the case those fundamental financial aspects that characterize the type.

By this account, the *a priori* conceptual framework allows the "intellectual seeing" of the type. Not only does the conceptual background deepen knowledge, but also it is necessary for knowledge. Compare that to Hayden White, for whom the *a priori* conceptual frameworks impair or prevent knowledge. They introduce subjectivity and lead to relativism. But White's argument presumes, like Mill, the "sterile" view that scientific inquiry requires only data and method. Instead, type induction explains historiography in which an informed mind thoroughly probes one historical case. Here is another central point. The implicit definitions of inductive reasoning underlying charges about the putative weakness of historiographical reasoning are sometimes inadequate.

The fifth account of induction, proposed by Whewell ([1850] 1989) in the mid-nineteenth century, presents another explanation for the discovery of inductive generalizations. Whewell defends Aristotle's "quite coherent and intelligible" account of induction (312). But he posits something different: the imaginative invention of hypotheses, which may be termed *inventive induction*.

During the first half of the nineteenth century, "hypothesis" was a pejorative term, signifying an unreasoned guess. Bacon generally held this view, and Mill tightly restricted the use of hypotheses, believing that they could not produce knowledge (Daniels 1968; Jardine 1974). In contrast, Whewell argues that the process of induction in scientific inquiry and discovery cannot be reduced to data and method. Hypotheses are necessary for the amplification of knowledge, and forming hypotheses requires imagination and invention.

Inductive generalizations originate in "the sagacity of discoverers. This sagacity cannot be taught. It commonly succeeds by guessing; and . . . a supply of appropriate hypotheses cannot be constructed by rule, nor without inventive talent" (1858, 59). Responding to Mill, Whewell writes, "the process of induction includes a mysterious step, by which we pass from particulars to generals" ([1849] 1989, 302).

During the nineteenth century, Mill's view predominated. The tide turned at the beginning of the twentieth century when philosophers of science, prompted by Peirce, began to favor Whewell's view (Putnam 1992, 276; Black 1972, 174, 180; Fisch 1991). By the mid-twentieth century, it was widely recognized that, in scientific research and, more generally, in academic research, "formulating or discovering relevant hypotheses is not a mechanical process but a creative one" (Copi 1972, 449; see Losee 1980, 83). For example, chemist James B. Conant, the president of Harvard University, embraced this view in the early 1950s, as Wayne Urban and Sarah Wever discuss in their essay.

Conant apparently conveyed this view to Thomas Kuhn, who served as a teaching assistant to Conant in his history of science course during the 1950s at Harvard, as Urban and Wever describe. In 1962, Kuhn then published his path-breaking book, *The Structure of Scientific Revolutions*, which philosophers regard as presenting an account of inductive discovery.[1] Kuhn's famous concept of "paradigm" in scientific research may be considered analogous to a theoretical framework underlying type induction. Kuhn's analysis of "when paradigms change," relying on "intuition," may be considered somewhat analogous to inventive induction, though Kuhn did not consider intuition unanalyzable or individual (1970, 111, 191).

In contrast, Hayden White maintains that literature is "inventive" and "imaginative," while science is "nomological-deductive" (1973, 6). Since historiography involves imagination and invention, it is literature and not science. Here again, White presupposes a "sterile" conception of scientific method that philosophers of science viewed as outdated. The nonscientific reasoning that he attributes to historiography and associates with fiction writing overlooks the complicated nature of induction.

CONCLUSION

In sum, this chapter argues that certain factors contribute to the perception of weakness in historical reasoning. These include:

- the indeterminacy and malleability of historical topics and questions
- the difficulty of finding and examining historical evidence
- the neglect of analyzing inductive reasoning
- the inherently provisional nature of inductive inferences
- the variability among kinds of inductive reasoning that fit different approaches to historical research
- the lack of consensus on one account of inductive discovery of hypotheses

Apart from the perception of weakness, the author responds as follows to the question of whether historical reasoning is actually weak. First, historiography is based on type and inventive induction, which require *a priori* and imaginative contributions of the historian. Second, science employs type and inventive induction, while literature also employs *a priori* and imaginative contributions of the author. Therefore, the author concludes that history, literature, and science all rely on *a priori* and imaginative contributions and cannot be distinguished in these grounds.[2]

Finally, the author would observe that this conclusion does not entail any claim that history is a science. Other distinctions may remain. For example, scientists conduct experiments, and historians generally cannot.

REFERENCES

Aristotle. 2002. *Posterior Analytics*. 2nd ed. Translated by Jonathan Barnes. Oxford: Oxford University Press.
Black, Max. 1972. "Induction." In *The Encyclopedia of Philosophy*. Vol. 4, edited by Paul Edwards, 169–81. New York: Macmillan.
Bozeman, Theodore D. 1977. *Protestants in an Age of Science: The Baconian Ideal and Antebellum American Religious Thought*. Chapel Hill: University of North Carolina Press.
Bruce, Robert V. 1987. *The Launching of Modern American Science, 1846–1876*. New York: Knopf.
Carr, David. 1986. *Time, Narrative, and History*. Bloomington: Indiana University Press.
Cohen, L. Jonathan. 1989. *An Introduction to the Philosophy of Induction and Probability*. Oxford: Clarendon.
Cohen, Morris R., and Ernest Nagel. 1934. *An Introduction to Logic and Scientific Method*. New York: Harcourt, Brace.
Copi, Irving M. 1972. *Introduction to Logic*. 4th ed. New York: Macmillan.
Cronon, William. 1992. "A Place for Stories: Nature, History, and Narrative." *Journal of American History* 78 (4): 1347–76.
Daniels, George H. 1968. *American Science in the Age of Jackson*. New York: Columbia University Press.
Dewey, John. 1912. "Induction and Deduction." In *A Cyclopedia of Education*. Vol. 3, edited by Paul Monroe, 422–24. New York: Macmillan.
Fisch, Menachem. 1991. *William Whewell: Philosopher of Science*. Oxford: Clarendon.
Fischer, David H. 1970. *Historians' Fallacies: Toward a Logic of Historical Thought*. New York: Harper and Row.
Ghiselin, Michael T. 1969. *The Triumph of the Darwinian Method*. Chicago: University of Chicago Press.
Herschel, John F. W. 1830. *A Preliminary Discourse on the Study of Natural Philosophy*. London: Longman.
Jardine, Lisa. 1974. *Francis Bacon: Discovery and the Art of Discourse*. Cambridge: Cambridge University Press.
Kansteiner, Wulf. 1993. "Hayden White's Critique of the Writing of History." *History and Theory* 32 (3): 273–95.
Kemeny, John G. 1963. "Carnap's Theory of Probability and Induction." In The Philosophy of Rudolf Carnap, edited by Paul Arthur Schilpp, 711–37. La Salle, IL: Open Court.
Kuhn, Thomas S. 1962. *The Structure of Scientific Revolutions*. Chicago: University of Chicago Press.
———. 1970. *The Structure of Scientific Revolutions*. 2nd ed. Chicago: University of Chicago Press.

Levisohn, John A. 2010. "Negotiating Historical Narratives: An Epistemology of History for History Education." *Journal of Philosophy of Education* 44 (1): 1–21.
Losee, John. 1980. *A Historical Introduction to the Philosophy of Science*. New ed. Oxford: Oxford University Press.
Mill, John S. 1874. *A System of Logic, Ratiocinative and Inductive*. 8th ed. New York: Harper.
Milton, J. R. 1987. "Induction before Hume." *British Journal of the Philosophy of Science* 38:49–74.
Paul, Hermann. 2011. *Hayden White: The Historical Imagination*. London: Polity.
Peirce, Charles S. 1931. "Ampliative Reasoning." In *Collected Papers of Charles Sanders Peirce*. Vol. 2, edited by Charles Hartshorne and Paul Weiss, 619–791. Cambridge, MA: Harvard University Press.
Peters, F. E. 1967. *Greek Philosophical Terms: A Historical Lexicon*. New York: New York University Press.
Putnam, Hilary. 1992. "Comments on the Lectures." In *Reasoning and the Logic of Things: The Cambridge Conferences Lectures of 1898*, edited by Kenneth L. Ketner, 55–102. Cambridge, MA: Harvard University Press.
Randall, John H. 1960. *Aristotle*. New York: Columbia University Press.
Ross, Dorothy. 1991. *The Origins of American Social Science*. Cambridge: Cambridge University Press.
Timmins, Adam. 2011. Review of *Hayden White: The Historical Imagination*. *Reviews in History* 1149 (October 1).http://www.history.ac.uk/reviews/review/1149.
Urbach, Peter. 1987. *Francis Bacon's Philosophy of Science: An Account and a Reappraisal*. LaSalle, IL: Open Court.
Vickers, Brian. 1992. "Francis Bacon and the Progress of Knowledge." *Journal of the History of Ideas* 53 (3): 495–518.
Whewell, William. (1849) 1989. "Mr. Mill's Logic." In *William Whewell's Theory of Scientific Method*, edited by Robert E. Butts (1968). Indianapolis: Hackett.
———. (1850) 1989. "Criticism of Aristotle's Account of Induction." In *William Whewell's Theory of Scientific Method*, edited by Robert E. Butts (1968), 311–21. Indianapolis: Hackett.
———. 1858. *Novum Organon Renovatum: Being the Second Part of the Philosophy of the Inductive Sciences*. London: John W. Parker.
White, Hayden. 1973. *Metahistory: The Historical Imagination in Nineteenth-Century Europe*. Baltimore: Johns Hopkins University Press.

NOTES

1. I am grateful to Bryan Warnick and Randy Curren for this insight, although my presentation may not adequately represent their own understanding.
2. I want to thank Doug Yacek for helping me to clarify the argument.

Chapter Three

The Mutual Intellectual Relationship of John Dewey and Ella Flagg Young

Contributions to Education *Series, 1901–1902*

Jackie M. Blount

Ella Flagg Young, fifty years old, walked into her first University of Chicago (UC) class in autumn of 1895. John Dewey, the highly recruited and recently hired professor of philosophy and pedagogy, taught the course, Philosophy 2: Introduction to Ethics (Donatelli 1971, 137–38; Dewey [1895] 1972, 291–301). For the next nine years, this soon-to-be world-renowned educational leader and this increasingly eminent philosopher would collaborate intensively, each profoundly affecting the thought of the other.

Young managed to carve only a few hours a week out of her demanding work as an assistant superintendent of Chicago's schools so she might attend Dewey's class. Right away, though, Young and Dewey took to each other. They vigorously discussed seminar topics—largely just with each other as they locked in lively debate—much to the chagrin of sidelined class members (McManis 1916, 102–3). He inspired her to develop her philosophical and theoretical understandings; she provoked him to better comprehend the deep complexities of urban schools—particularly at a time when women dominated the work of teaching, were just beginning to assume significant school leadership positions, and yet were denied such fundamentally important powers as the vote.

Their interactions intensified as Young continued her studies. Eventually, Dewey guided her through completion of her dissertation. At the behest of both Dewey and UC president William Rainey Harper, she then joined the faculty in the Department of Education, working alongside Dewey on many projects, including the famed Laboratory School (McManis 1916; Smith

1979). Their multifaceted intellectual collaboration culminated in 1901 and 1902 with the publication of a six-monograph series collected in the single volume, *Contributions to Education* (University of Chicago Press).

Professors Dewey and Young worked together in numerous other ways, too. For example, they helped each other navigate administrative frustrations during their years at UC. Dewey intervened on Young's behalf whenever President Harper reneged on commitments to her. In turn, Young worked feverishly in the background to resolve Dewey's brewing conflicts with Laboratory School teachers, patrons, and interested community members. Dewey famously resigned in 1904 to accept the Columbia University philosophy position that he would hold for the remainder of his career. Almost certainly acting in sympathy, Young submitted her resignation letter only weeks after Dewey's. They went their separate ways (Smith 1979).

Then in 1909, worldwide newswires carried the stunning news that Chicago officials had appointed Young to serve as superintendent, the first woman chosen for such a high public position in the United States, in schools or otherwise. A year later, she became the first woman elected president of the National Education Association (NEA), furthering her position as one of the most esteemed educators of her day—at any level. As Young focused her attention on practical matters in her leadership roles, her years of intellectual engagement with Dewey continued to manifest in some ways (Smith 1979; McManis 1916).

After Dewey moved to Columbia University, he followed Young's career with great interest. However, as Ellen Condliffe Lagemann has argued, he turned his intellectual focus away from the immediacies of schools and teachers even as he later wrote *Democracy and Education* (1916) and other works (Lagemann 1996). Nonetheless, his thinking had been enriched by his work with Young. Dewey's daughter later recounted that he regarded "Mrs. Young as the wisest person in school matters with whom he has come in contact in any way.... Contact with her supplemented Dewey's educational ideas where his own experience was lacking in matters of practical administration, crystallizing his ideas of democracy in the school and, by extension, in life" ([Jane] Dewey 1939, 29).

In the end, Young and Dewey's *Contributions to Education* volume remains one of the clearest and most important scholarly expressions of their collaboration—and as such, is the focus of this chapter. The volume initially attracted an attentive readership. Then in the following decades, Dewey's influence further developed while he cultivated a reputation as a public intellectual of the first order. His works have since been reprinted many times; the Center for Dewey Studies was established, which contains much of his correspondence and other personal documents; and outstanding biographies about him have been published (Westbrook 1991; Martin 2002).

Young's work *Isolation in the School* was hailed at the time by the venerable Margaret Haley, a leader of the Chicago Teachers' Federation, as "the bible of the teachers of the United States" and generally was prized across the country as a manifesto for teacher empowerment (Haley 1935, 198–99). However, after Illinois granted women full suffrage in 1913, a powerful backlash movement specifically targeted Young, the most prominent woman in public service. Young, an intensely private person, left quietly at the end of 1915. She did not preserve any of her personal records, compile her published works, or otherwise promote her legacy. In the decades following her death in 1918, her scholarship was all but forgotten. When scholars remembered her, they typically attributed her ideas to Dewey without crediting either her original thought or the importance of Young and Dewey's mutual influence.

This chapter briefly examines Dewey and Young's experiences and publications predating the *Contributions to Education* volume. Then it describes some of the ways that Dewey and Young each acknowledge the influence of the other in these six monographs. Finally, the chapter offers a few closing thoughts on the importance of historically situating these works—especially as Young's influential voice essentially has been lost. With this, arguably, we may have missed much of what notably animated Dewey's deep interest in education generally—and schools specifically.

HISTORICAL CONTEXT

The ambitious UC president William Rainey Harper aggressively recruited Dewey to lead the Department of Philosophy and Pedagogy. However, he did not offer the $7,000 salary Dewey had wanted, the salary bestowed on the university's most prized faculty hires. Instead, Harper offered $5,000 and sweetened the deal by suggesting that Dewey create an experimental school. Furthermore, Harper explained that he had already planned to take over one nearby school for such a purpose (Dewey 1939, 27; McCaul 1959, 260; Cruikshank 1998, 386). Harper thought this might appeal because, after all, Dewey had been a teacher.

Dewey, though, had been a reluctant teacher. When other prospects failed to materialize, his cousin, a high-school principal, offered him his first job (Martin 2002, 46–50; Eastman 1941, 672–73). Dewey taught for two years, but his contract was not renewed after his cousin departed (Knoll 2014, 4–5). He then taught high school south of Burlington, Vermont, where a former student said about his undistinguished teaching: "How terribly the boys behaved, and how long and fervent was the prayer with which he opened each school day" (quoted in Westbrook 1991, 8). When Dewey enrolled in graduate school at Johns Hopkins a year later, he was spared further torment in the school classroom.

Despite his limited and unremarkable teaching experience, Dewey nonetheless was enticed by the pedagogical aspects of Harper's offer of an experimental school because, as he explained to his wife, Alice: "My additional scheme was not simply to train teachers for colleges & high schools—in fact, I didn't care much about that, but Supts who could train their own teachers, & [sic] to organize a complete experimental school under our control in order to do this" (quoted in Cruikshank 1998, 386). He further elaborates that an important attraction of the experimental school is that the Deweys' own children could attend it. Dewey would later hire Alice Dewey to serve as principal of the Laboratory School, though her own teaching experience, too, had been quite limited.[1]

Finally, before Harper's offer, Dewey had published exceedingly little work concerning schools or education, including just these four articles: "Education and the Health of Women," "Health and Sex in Higher Education," "Psychology in High Schools from the Standpoint of the College," and "Teaching Ethics in the High School" (Boydston 1969, 1971). None of these works reveals an interest in or deep understanding of schools, particularly urban or experimental schools. In the end, though, Dewey happily accepted Harper's offer in 1894. A year later, he began writing and publishing extensively about schools and education—the same year he came to know Ella Flagg Young (Boydston 1972).

Before Young took her first course with Dewey, she already had achieved a highly distinguished thirty-three-year career with the Chicago schools. Reputedly no one in the city knew more about schools than Young. Remarkably, she had dropped out of school after only a few months, citing intense boredom. She taught herself to read, though, and quickly became a voracious reader. Then at age fifteen, she easily passed the teachers' examination but was not allowed to teach because she had not attended school long enough.

She enrolled in the Chicago Normal Program, but to address what she regarded as her own lack of classroom experience, she created a unique, extensive practice-teaching program with a mentor she had befriended. When she began teaching in one of the city's most challenging schools and classes, she brought unconventional, self-devised approaches to working with students—approaches that succeeded to such a remarkable degree that she earned a series of rapid promotions (Smith 1979; McManis 1916).

In part, she succeeded by establishing a strict, self-disciplined practice of devoting several nights each week to careful professional study as well as extensive readings in philosophy, history, and literature, a practice she maintained throughout her career. Within a few years, she became principal of the new School of Practice, charged with preparing teachers for this rapidly growing city system. Then she was promoted to principal of an entire school, one of the first handful of women school principals anywhere in the country.

She attracted national fame when the noted education journalist A. E. Winship, on a tour of hundreds of schools across the country, wrote about her and mentioned her frequently in his many speeches, describing her as the finest teacher he had ever encountered (example: Winship 1905, 250–51). In the wake of this attention, the school board selected Young to become an assistant superintendent, again one of the first women in the country to hold such a position.

In her new leadership role, Young delivered at least a half dozen papers at professional conferences that were subsequently published (examples: 1888, 1889, and 1892). She brought to her writings a striking combination of both practical understanding as well as theoretical conception, original thinking, and willingness to fundamentally rethink conventional wisdom. In short, she demonstrated a notable scholarly capacity.

CONTRIBUTIONS TO EDUCATION

By the time Dewey and Young published *Contributions to Education*, Young had defended her dissertation (1900), served for a year as an associate professor, and then speedily achieved promotion to full professor in 1901 (Smith 1979). Young and Dewey clearly wanted to publish together. Dewey may have wanted to help his former doctoral student, current colleague, and friend build her scholarly portfolio and attract a broader readership. Young may have wanted to demonstrate that she had learned well from her major professor.

Also, she may have wanted to prove her scholarly mettle, to show that she was a deserving member of the vibrant philosophy and education faculty that William James would later proclaim had created the "Chicago School of Thought" (University of Chicago 1903; James 1904, 1). In the end, Young and Dewey published a work that reflected their intellectual debts to the other. The following are brief descriptions of each monograph, including suggestive discussions of their mutual influence.

Number 1. *Isolation in the School* (Young 1901)

Young's doctoral dissertation (1900), republished in the *Contributions to Education* series, offers a theoretical analysis of the leadership she practiced during the decades she served as principal and assistant superintendent, leadership that empowered students and teachers alike. She argues strenuously against increasingly centralized and hierarchical school administrative practice. Furthermore, she contends that schools succeed to the extent that true cooperation is fostered. Otherwise, there is a default tendency toward "isolation" among the many parts of the educational enterprise, such as compartmentalized organization, imperfect communication, and disempowerment of individuals who are discouraged from exercising free thought and social discourse.

Her final chapter includes a detailed discussion of a concrete means of instituting truly democratic processes in schools and essentially empowering teachers—teachers' councils—much as she had implemented a decade earlier as an assistant superintendent.

In *Isolation in the School*, Young frames her understandings in scholarly terms. She opens with a thesis statement and then carefully develops the precise language and boundaries of her arguments, gradually building a larger, sweeping exploration of a battle between "isolation" and empowerment in school leadership. As Dewey puts it, "What Mrs. Young got from her study of philosophy was chiefly a specific intellectual point of view and terminology . . . in which to clear up and express the practical outcome of her prior experience" (McManis 1916, 119).

Number 2. *Psychology and Social Practice* (Dewey 1901)

In this monograph, first delivered as his presidential address before the American Psychological Association (APA) in 1899, Dewey describes the relationship of the field of psychology to education. Beyond attempting to understand the unique psychological characteristics of adults and children as they may affect education, he explains that it is also essential to understand that there is a difference in "the conditions which secure intellectual and moral progress and power" (12).

Adults typically are thought to have power to originate ideas and realize their personal ends. Conversely, children, who are expected to be passive recipients of preformed ideas and lack opportunities for experimentation and free thought, are effectively stunted in realizing their full powers. Dewey provides a note to this grounding idea, stating in both the original APA as well as the *Contributions* versions, that: "I owe this point specifically (as well as others more generally) to my friend and colleague, Mrs. Ella Flagg Young" (n. 12). He continues, explaining that when teachers are treated as servile, they essentially lose their capacities for free, original thought—which in turn affects their ability to nurture these qualities in their students. This line of reasoning aligns with the central arguments of Young's *Isolation in the School*.

Number 3. *The Educational Situation* (Dewey 1902b)

Dewey unites three previously published works that explore conditions of education at the elementary, secondary, and college levels. He identifies common aspects of the "educational situation," including a tendency toward "isolation" in all aspects of schooling, including curriculum, grade divisions, school levels, and differentiated levels of power among educators, all of which build upon Young's notion of "isolation."

To make this connection clear, Dewey only offers two notes in this entire 104-page monograph—both of them citing Young's *Isolation in the School*. He explains: "The unity and wholeness of the child's development can be realized only in a corresponding unity and continuity of school conditions. Anything that breaks the latter up into fractions, into isolated parts, must have the same influence upon the educative growth of the child" (26 and n.1).

He then offers a parallel argument concerning the empowerment/disempowerment of teachers, again drawing on *Isolation*: "As long as the teacher, who is after all the only real educator in the school system, has no definite and authoritative position in shaping the course of study, that is likely to remain an external thing to be externally applied to the child" (30–31 and n. 1). In the end, there is a tendency, he argues, toward the disempowerment of students and teachers alike—which separates humans from their capacity for free thought, rather than "changing school conditions so as to make real the aims that command the assent of our intelligence and the support of our moral enthusiasm" (49).

Number 4. *Ethics in the School* (Young 1902a)

Young's monograph, *Ethics in the School*, is intended to assist teachers in their classroom practice, a feat she accomplishes through her choice of practical topics as well as accessible writing. She explains that teachers need to fundamentally rethink their unconsidered assumptions about the ends of schooling. She argues against then-pervasive views that students must learn to imitate and produce work conforming to certain standards; that competition is necessary to compel students to attain those standards; and that teachers may need to employ corporal punishment, sarcasm, and other forms of verbal punishment.

Young argues instead that teachers should encourage students to interpret, to bring uniqueness to their assignments, to play with ideas, and to arrive at their own understandings. Teachers at their best should strive to understand the individual qualities of their students. In short, teachers should grant students freedom to be individuals while empowering them through democratic processes, which Young had long practiced as teacher, principal, and assistant superintendent—before she had ever met Dewey.

Number 5. *The Child and the Curriculum* (Dewey 1902a)

Dewey begins this monograph by describing a seemingly irresolvable dichotomy in educational thought at the time: that, on the one hand, a child should dutifully absorb a carefully sequenced, predigested curriculum designed to cover a particular subject and, on the other hand, a child's desires and inclinations should guide all instruction. He explains that such polarized thinking is irreconcilable.

Instead, questions about children and curriculum need to be enlarged beyond the limitations of such narrow dichotomies. He argues for the importance of give-and-take between student and teacher as well as for the necessity for guidance, not "external imposition" (22). Though Dewey does not specifically reference Young in this monograph, his significant discussion of how teachers might guide students' development clearly is inspired by Young, as he later explains: "I hardly ever have seen anybody who had such an habitual and keen sense of the influence of one person's associations with others upon mental habits as had Mrs. Young. And I have never seen anyone with such a keen sense of it as applied to classroom procedure—the reflex effect of the teacher's habits upon the pupil in all kinds of subtle but pervasive ways. As a consequence, her sense of intellectual life as a 'give-and-take' process was practically instinctive" (McManis 1916, 121). Arguably, Dewey describes Young, the teacher, in *The Child and the Curriculum*.

Number 6. *Some Types of Educational Theory* (Young 1902b)

Young wrote *Some Types of Modern Educational Theory* to commemorate what she regarded as an important shift in the educational field toward "the introduction of scientific method into its modes of experimentation and generalization." She analyzes the works of five education scholars, including Dewey, who had brought to their work some degree of scientific analysis.

She holds out Dewey's approach as the most significant, admiring his scientific inquiry where, "instead of drawing up a scheme, a theory, to which all facts and conditions in school life must conform, he seeks a working hypothesis and tests it by its efficiency in explaining the familiar and the unexpected which are projected into the foreground of the field of observation and practice in which the teacher operates. The hypothesis gives a method of investigation, not a fixed ideal" (54–55). Young essentially embraces Dewey's emerging style of scientific inquiry in educational theory and practice.

DEWEY CREDITS YOUNG

John McManis, a former UC student of both Dewey and Young, published a biography of Young in 1916, just after she left the Chicago superintendency. Dewey contributed a lengthy letter to the project, describing that he thought Young had gained from her doctoral studies "a specific intellectual point of view and terminology," largely scientific in orientation, which had allowed her to possess "a greater command of her experience and a greater intellectual assurance." He continues modestly, "This led her in many respects to overestimate the explicit content of my own teachings. That is, she gave me credit for seeing all of the bearings and implications which *she* with her experience and outlook got out of what I said" (McManis 1916, 119).

Conversely, Dewey attempts to describe the magnitude of what *he* got from *her*: "Regarding my relations to Mrs. Young: . . . it is hard to be specific, because they were so continuous and so detailed that the influence resulting from them was largely insensible. I was constantly getting ideas from her." He notes that, "She had by temperament and training the gist of a concrete empirical pragmatism with reference to philosophical conceptions before the doctrine was ever formulated in print. . . . Apart from the suggestions, which were so numerous that I couldn't name them, what I chiefly got from Mrs. Young was just the translation of philosophic conceptions into their empirical equivalents."

Furthermore, he often "didn't see the meaning or force of some favorite conception of my own till Mrs. Young had given it back to me." And given her "keen sense" of the give-and-take, the social possibilities of the classroom, he offers a stunning intellectual attribution: "I owe chiefly to association with Mrs. Young the depth of my conviction that all psychology which isn't physiological is social." Dewey concludes by comparing Theodore Roosevelt with Young: "I often think that Roosevelt's knowledge of politics is the only analog of Mrs. Young's knowledge of educational matters with which I am acquainted. And I should be inclined to guess that the latter's was the more reflective of the two" (119–22).

Though Dewey spoke freely about Young's influence on his thought—and readily credited her, eventually her contributions and their collaboration were largely forgotten. Scholars began attributing Young's ideas to Dewey, for example, as George Counts did in his classic volume *The School and Society in Chicago*, where he incorrectly states that Dewey had inspired Young to create teachers' councils when she was superintendent (1928, 110). Instead, Young's teachers' councils had predated any connection with Dewey—and it was she who had compelled him to understand the importance of teacher empowerment in schools. Nonetheless, work such as Counts's was cited and re-cited through scholarly generations as Young's fragile volumes crumbled on shelves.

In a final effort to restore her scholarly place, Young's long-time companion, Laura Brayton, attempted to have Young's writings collected and published posthumously. Brayton and Dewey corresponded about the possibility that he might edit such a volume. She explained to him, "This arrangement seemed to me the ideal one and the one Mrs. Young herself [would] choose above all others" (Brayton 1924). Dewey then attempted to secure a contract to publish Young's work but never succeeded. One rejection letter he received from a publisher explained that there did not seem to be a market for such a book, despite Dewey's involvement (Walsh 1930).

Ella Flagg Young's intellectual contributions are not the only ones submerged in the historical record. As Jane Roland Martin poignantly describes in her contemporary classic *Reclaiming a Conversation* (1985), twentieth-century philosophers of education largely have ignored women. As I argue in this chapter, though, Ella Flagg Young's ideas are worthy of understanding in their own right. However, they also are quite important because of their foundational influence on the man who has come to be known perhaps as the world's most influential modern educational philosopher.

Dewey's philosophical concern for education and schools was minimal until he came to UC and began significantly collaborating with Young, who tutored him persistently in matters of education while he in turn mentored her philosophical inquiry. When Dewey and Young parted, his interest in education grew more abstract and disconnected from the immediacies of schools—and concern for teachers. Undoubtedly, Young's intellectual contributions—in general as well as to Dewey's thought—would be better understood were the entirety of her published work compiled and made easily accessible. To this end, I am preparing such a compilation to accompany an extensive biography of Young (forthcoming). Until then, *Contributions to Education* offers an important window into their rich intellectual collaboration.

REFERENCES

Boydston, Jo Ann, ed. 1969. *John Dewey: The Early Works, 1882–1888*. Vol. 1. Carbondale: University of Southern Illinois Press.

———, ed. 1971. *John Dewey: The Early Works, 1882–1888*. Vol. 4. Carbondale: University of Southern Illinois Press.

———, ed. 1972. *John Dewey: The Early Works, 1882*–1888. Vol. 5. Carbondale: University of Southern Illinois Press.

Brayton, Laura. 1924. Letter from Laura T. Brayton to John Dewey. June 8, 1924. John Dewey Papers 7/5. Center for Dewey Studies, Carbondale, IL.

Counts, George. 1928. *School and Society in Chicago*. New York: Harcourt, Brace.

Cruikshank, Kathleen. 1998. "In Dewey's Shadow: Julia Bulkley and the University of Chicago Department of Pedagogy, 1895–1900." *History of Education Quarterly* 38 (4): 373–406.

Dewey, Jane. 1939. "Biography of John Dewey." In *The Philosophy of John Dewey*, edited by Paul Arthur Schilpp, 3–45. New York: Tudor.

Dewey, John [1895] 1972. "Educational Ethics: Syllabus of a Course of Six Lecture-Studies." In John Dewey: The Early Works, 1882–1898, Vol. 5. Edited by Jo Anne Boydston, 291–301. Carbondale and Edwardsville, IL: Southern Illinois University Press.

———. 1901. "Psychology and Social Practice." *Contributions to Education*, no. 2. Chicago: University of Chicago Press.

———. 1902a. "The Child and the Curriculum." *Contributions to Education*, no. 5. Chicago: University of Chicago Press.

———. 1902b. "The Educational Situation." *Contributions to Education*, no. 3. Chicago: University of Chicago Press.

———. 1916. *Democracy and Education: An Introduction to the Philosophy of Education*. New York: Macmillan.

Donatelli, Rosemary. 1971. "The Contributions of Ella Flagg Young to the Educational Enterprise." PhD diss., University of Chicago.

Eastman, Max. 1941. "John Dewey." *Atlantic Monthly* 168 (December): 672–73.

Haley, Margaret. 1935. Autobiography. Manuscript. Box 34, folder. Chicago Teachers Federation Collection. Chicago Historical Museum.

James, William. 1904. "The Chicago School." *Psychological Bulletin* 1 (January 15): 1–5.

Knoll, Michael. 2014. "John Dewey as Administrator: The Inglorious End of the Laboratory School in Chicago." *Journal of Curriculum Studies* (August): 1–50. doi:10.1080/00220272.2014.936045.

Lagemann, Ellen Condliffe. 1996. "Experimenting with Education: John Dewey and Ella Flagg Young at the University of Chicago." *American Journal of Education* 104 (May): 171–85.

McCaul, Robert. 1959. "Dewey's Chicago." *The School Review* 67, 2: 258–80.

McManis, John T. 1916. *Ella Flagg Young and a Half Century of the Chicago Public Schools*. Chicago: McClurg.

Martin, Jane Roland. 1985. *Reclaiming a Conversation: The Ideal of the Educated Woman*. New Haven, CT: Yale University Press.

Martin, Jay. 2002. *The Education of John Dewey: A Biography*. New York: Columbia University Press.

Smith, Joan K. 1979. *Ella Flagg Young: Portrait of a Leader*. Ames, IA: Educational Studies Press and the Iowa State University Research Foundation.

Stack, Sam. 2009. "Alice Chipman Dewey (1858–1927): Still a Mystery?" *Journal of Philosophy and History of Education* 59:28–37.

University of Chicago. 1903. *Decennial Publications*. First series, vol. 3, part 2. Chicago: University of Chicago Press.

Walsh, Richard. 1930. Letter from Richard J. Walsh to John Dewey. July 24. John Dewey Papers. John Day Archives 38/48, used with permission of Princeton University Library. Center for Dewey Studies, Carbondale, IL.

Westbrook, Robert. 1991. *John Dewey and American Democracy*. Ithaca, NY: Cornell University Press.

Winship, A. E. 1905. "Mrs. Ella Flagg Young." *Journal of Education* (August 31): 250–51.

Young, Ella Flagg. 1888. "How to Teach Parents to Discriminate between Good and Bad Teaching." *Journal of Proceedings and Addresses of the National Educational Association* 1887:245–49. Salem, MA: NEA.

———. 1889. "System in Education." *Intelligence* 9 (April 1): 101–3.

———. 1892. "Classic Study in Our Public Schools." *Intelligence* 12 (November 15): 279–80.

———. 1901. "Isolation in the School." *Contributions to Education*. Vol. 1. Chicago: University of Chicago Press. Original edition 1900.

———. 1902a. "Ethics in the School." *Contributions to Education*. Vol. 4. Chicago: University of Chicago Press.

———. 1902b. "Some Types of Modern Educational Theory." *Contributions to Education*. Vol. 6. Chicago: University of Chicago Press.

———. 1903. "Scientific Method in Education." In University of Chicago, *Decennial Publications*. First series, vol. 3, part 2, 143–55. Chicago: University of Chicago Press.

NOTE

1. Alice Dewey taught high school in Flushing, Michigan, for a few years before enrolling at the University of Michigan in 1883 (Stack 2009, 28–29). Before moving to Chicago, she had no experience teaching children at the primary level, the level of the Laboratory School over which she would serve as principal.

Chapter Four

Blending the Philosophy and the History of Education

Discussions of the Works of Boyd Bode, Bernard Mehl, and Maxine Greene

Joseph Watras

Editors' note: Joe Watras, one of the rare scholars to devote his work to the history and philosophy of education—as well as to their interrelationship—passed away as authors drafted their chapters for this book. We are grateful to Christina Watras for granting us permission to publish Joe's manuscript posthumously.

The standards of the Council for Social Foundations of Education (CSFE) state the connection that should exist between the historical and philosophical study of education. According to those standards, the disciplines of the humanities, particularly history and philosophy, should help educators develop interpretive, normative, and critical perspectives about education (CSFE 2014, 110, 111).

The field grew from George Counts's book *The Social Foundations of Education*, published in 1934 by the American Historical Society (AHA) as the ninth contribution out of fourteen major volumes by the AHA's Commission on the Social Studies. Although the commission sought to determine the role of the social sciences in schools, Counts recognized that educators had to make concrete choices about teachers, subject matters, and textbooks. He argued that in making these choices teachers had to consider the beneficial theories of government and appropriate values. Counts added it was the task of social scientists to inform teachers about the theories and values. He noted that society was becoming less individualistic and more collectivistic and described different ways educators could think about advancing democracy in light of these changing times (Counts 1934, 532–63).

Although several scholars followed Counts's model, three individuals illustrate the ways to blend history and philosophy in ways that reduce educational confusion. Boyd Bode devoted attention to the tendencies of psychologists and curriculum theorists to develop a science of teaching. He complained that their efforts failed because they ignored questions about the aim of education. Bode was a trained logician, and he was sensitive to the shallow thinking that resulted when educators ignored philosophy. Bernard Mehl was a historian by training. He used history to reveal the philosophical ideas that dominated American culture. Maxine Greene was trained as a philosopher of education. She was able to use her love of literature to blend philosophy and history of education to illuminate the complex problems in American society. The sections that follow will explain these points more fully.

BOYD BODE: PHILOSOPHY TO REDUCE PROBLEMS PSYCHOLOGISTS HISTORICALLY IGNORED

In the preface of *Fundamentals of Education*, Bode explained that the purpose of his work was to revitalize educational theory. Popular educational researchers applied a superficial model of scientific thinking to solve educational problems. They used science to achieve shallow ends. They made schools more mechanical, and they made it difficult for the teachers who followed their models to enlighten students (Bode 1921, v–vi).

Bode showed the dangers of a misapplication of science by tracing the development of various educational theories. In *Fundamentals of Education*, he criticized theories of transfer of training, the notion of the soul as the motive for learning, the doctrine of mental states, and consciousness as behavior. In describing the Herbartian effort to train students to think, he showed that the five formal steps could not achieve this aim because the model failed to give students a sense of a problem to be solved (Bode 1921, 126–44).

Bode noted that science advanced one way to consider educational problems, but philosophy brought another approach. Science may focus on efficiency, but ideas about aims or ideals came from philosophy. Bode contended that philosophy could help people evaluate the ideals they had held in the past and point to aims to make life more beautiful and people more human (Bode 1921, 224–42).

To make these points clearer, Bode evaluated five popular models of curriculum making in his next book, *Modern Educational Theories*. These included the logical and psychological organization of subject matter, Franklin Bobbitt's method of scientific analysis of community needs, W. W. Charter's method of job analysis, David Snedden's sociological determination of curriculum, and William Heard Kilpatrick's project method. Bode complained that the curriculum makers used science to justify these plans, but they repeated the evils of the traditional system (Bode 1927).

Two years after publishing *Modern Educational Theories*, Bode returned to analyses of psychological concepts in *Conflicting Psychologies of Learning*. In this book, Bode offered a historical account of the ways that psychologists showed the relation of the mind and the body. He contended that scientists lacked a theory about the nature of the mind and this caused them several problems (Bode 1929).

When Bode revised this book, he entitled it *How We Learn*. In the new volume, Bode repeated that educators exploring the problem of learning had to consider the nature of the mind. Bode described four distinct theories of the mind that illustrated the historical development of psychology. Only John Dewey's pragmatism presented a new perspective on educational theory and practice (Bode 1940).

The problem with the other theories was that psychologists held the body and mind to be qualitatively distinct. They considered a person's body to be material that was subject to the laws of physics; however, they conceived of the person's mind to belong to something that was independent of physical laws. When philosophers considered minds as souls or states of consciousness, their thinking led to inadequate views of education. For example, Bode argued that John Locke decided that the mind extracted qualities from particular objects, shaped them into representatives of general categories, and developed them into universals. If the mind undertook these activities, the appropriate method of education was to train the mind to see objects as concepts and to develop the mental capacities of memory, imagination, and judgment. Such ideas led to the creation of the object method that depended on memorization (Bode 1940, 8–10, 19–35).

Bode claimed that the modern form of materialism was behaviorism, which claimed that a reflex arc tied a stimulus to a reaction. According to behaviorists, such as Edward Lee Thorndike, this simple mechanism could explain complicated states of mind and emotions because the reactions became habits and the process of learning became a process of conditioning. Although Bode agreed that behavior came from experience, he thought that people could use their intelligence to make choices.

Thorndike did not believe that intelligence played a role in determining behavior. To illustrate his views, Bode borrowed a model from Albert Einstein's and Leopold Infeld's *The Evolution of Physics* to illuminate the path from experience to mind. According to Bode, the contribution of Einstein and Infeld was the theory that any object extended as far as its gravitational field. Matter was where the concentration of energy was great, and the field was where the concentration was less. This idea linked an object with the surrounding space (Bode 1940, 176–90, 213–15).

Bode created a similar model to explain behavior without referring to something called "consciousness." This idea had fallen into disrepute. Further, the notion of the mind as a field made it unnecessary to construct theories of learning where the mind was separate from the body. For example, Bode argued that the perceiving body was part of the field, and it was in action from the beginning of the perception process. In this way, he followed Dewey who had pointed out earlier that hearing a sound did not initiate a response; the hearing took place because a response was underway (Bode 1940, 226–30).

Bode contended that the idea of the mind as a field amplified Dewey's view that the mind progressively shaped the environment so that the activity concluded successfully. For example, an infant who placed a finger on a hot stove and suffered a burn might see the relationship between the stove and heat as part of an effort to predict what would happen in the future; however, Bode warned that the child could see the stove as something that burned, something that was bad, or something adults used. The differences in these meanings shaped the ways people would use stoves (Bode 1940, 231–36).

From these observations, Bode noted that the relationships people created through experiences became meanings that were part of the stimulus. Since the meanings people associated with the objects could take various directions, education could enrich and broaden those meanings. This was the point where intelligence and freedom could function. For example, schools could help students reconstruct their social experiences so they could move in the direction of the Golden Rule (Bode 1940, 241–47).

BERNARD MEHL: HISTORY TO REVEAL THE PHILOSOPHIC ORIENTATIONS OF AMERICAN EDUCATORS

Mehl worked in a different direction from Bode. While Bode considered philosophy as the tool and the psychological theories as the historical pattern that philosophy could clarify, Mehl used history as a tool to illuminate the cultural meanings implicit in educational theories.

Writing about the history of American education, Mehl focused on five major phases: the Puritan experience, the Enlightenment and the Revolution, the Jacksonian movement, the quest for social justice, and the modern economy. Mehl's aim was to use descriptions of education during these periods to illuminate the wider cultural meanings that had resulted (Mehl 1963).

In describing Puritan ideology, Mehl claimed its fatal flaw was that it depended on faith rather than piety. Holding to the Calvinistic doctrine of predestination, Puritans decided they could not influence God through prayer. Although they kept alive the idea that a moral element should pervade people's affairs, the Puritans looked to the law court and the schools to protect society from deviant thoughts and actions. The problem was that these mechanisms were too weak to maintain a stable society in the face of the many opportunities for material progress in the new country (Mehl 1963, 2–9).

Mehl explained that since Puritanism tried to use education as a means of strengthening faith, each specific branch within the colony established a college to reinforce its interpretations. They thought that schools could help people recognize the orderly world God revealed in the Bible. Although these colleges excluded science from the curriculum, elements that conflicted with religion came into the course of studies through Latin and Greek and weakened the theocratic state. As the purpose of compulsory education dissipated, the new republic reinforced feelings of individualism as people wrested personal wealth from the expanding frontier (Mehl 1963, 11–17).

The important aspect of Mehl's interpretation was that he argued there was no sharp conflict in which advocates of one form of education or beliefs rejected entirely a previous model. Instead, the supporters of each new form built on some aspect of the previous one. In the case of Puritanism, the capitalist state grew on an adulterated version of the Puritan faith in education as Benjamin Franklin advocated a form of vocational education that rewarded the members of the elect.

In his conclusion, Mehl referred to this tendency as loose pluralism that dulled the sharp aspects of most controversies. For example, he predicted that the then-current conflict over racial integration of schools would devolve into policies admitting some African Americans into some schools. This did not mean the problem was in the schools. According to Mehl, the difficulty was the acceptance of loose pluralism as the model of progress (Mehl 1963, 41).

In his book *Classical Educational Ideas*, Mehl maintained his concern for American cultural perspectives. He wrote that he had fused educational theory and history to form what he called the "educational imagination." For him, history was the tool that would locate the dynamics of the American culture. He called the book "one man's exploration into the vast field of education using history as a focus. The book departs from recent efforts by educators who insist on greater structure, focus, detachment and precision as a way out of educational confusion. Instead, it asks for more personal involvement based on deep thought and understanding" (Mehl 1972, vii).

Prominent historian Richard Hofstadter had expressed a similar view. When Hofstadter described his book *Anti-intellectualism in American Life*, he called it a "distinctly personal book." Hofstadter explained that he had directed the facts toward his theme in idiosyncratic ways (Hofstadter 1963, vii). When Mehl reviewed Maxine Greene's book *Public School Private*

Vision, he suggested that Hofstadter's method was one that educational historians should utilize.

Mehl praised Greene for making history a relevant experience for students who were wondering about the direction of their lives. He recognized that such an approach broke chronology, weakened continuity, and played havoc with traditional history; however, he believed that it could lead an author, such as Greene, to make creative insights in the fashion of Frederick Jackson Turner or Charles Austin Beard (Mehl 1966).

Mehl thought the history of education could illuminate the dynamics of the culture because education shaped social life. According to Mehl, civilized humans depended on education rather than environmental and biological laws. Of course, education took place within a historical context, and this provided the direction for the changes that were possible. For example, in America, transformations moved toward freedom because the democratic heritage supported such changes. Mehl predicted the drive for freedom had such deep roots that it could resist the efforts of reformers who would reduce human freedoms to make the world safer, cleaner, or better. Nonetheless, human beings could move beyond many historical strictures provided that they recognized the ecology within which the new thoughts had to meld. These were the limits within which they could move. In *Classical Educational Ideas*, he tried to define those limits (Mehl 1972, 1–8).

According to Mehl, when people formed a civilization, they moved away from thinking in terms of the existing environment and toward using abstract relationships. This meant that education led people away from the awareness of reality into artificially created world views. These world views gave them symbols with which they controlled the environment, created technologies, and organized education.

The difference between societies that seemed primitive and those called civilized came from the movement from simple direct experience to abstract thinking. The shift from primitive to civilized fell along a continuum characterized by the extent they limited value choices. Primitive societies had to restrict value choices to fit the world of experience; they rejected innovations. As other options appeared, societies tended to force people to adhere to one view. Finally, as options became appealing, a society tended to allow modifications in less important values while holding others central and immutable. This was similar to the idea of loose pluralism that Mehl defined earlier (Mehl 1972, 9–21).

In subsequent chapters, Mehl took readers through various epochs or periods. In the chapter on education in ancient Greece, Mehl described three alternatives that offered increasingly open models of truth. Plato's school tried to teach students to use dialectics to discover the truths that governed people's actions in the world. Aristotle modified this approach and asked students to discover the truth that existed in the world of experience. While

Plato's method depended on intuition, Aristotle encouraged the use of logic and analysis. The most prominent method was that of Isocrates who trained people in the art of rhetoric. Although Isocrates lacked any objective measures of truth, it made students aware of the exemplary models of art, music, and literature. Armed with such knowledge, these students became the leaders of society (Mehl 1972, 29–55).

Mehl's descriptions of each period had more to do with contemporary American education than with the era under study. For example, when Mehl described Roman education, he noted that the Romans borrowed the Greek models but turned literacy toward the bureaucratic requirements of the state. Accordingly, Isocrates's version of rhetoric became popular; however, the Romans transformed it into the seven liberal arts that served all professions. Mehl drew two conclusions relevant to American education. One was that educators might dilute knowledge if applied to a range of problems including personal ones. Another was the expansion of education leading to universal literacy could open avenues for the manipulation of the population. Although conservatives contend that educational changes weakened Roman civilization, Mehl pointed out that this could not have happened because the liberal arts fell when the Roman state did (Mehl 1972, 57–81).

Mehl found three different archetypes that typified the epochs he had discussed: the hero, the saint, and the artist. The hero portrayed the ideal of Greece and Rome as a warrior who could outwit the enemies of the tribe. During the Christian upheaval, the saint turned the pride of the hero into the strength of the saint as he or she struggled against temptation and sin. These types merged into the artist during the Renaissance as people sought to shape the world into works of art (Mehl 1972, 109–17).

Mehl used these archetypes to illustrate the strength of the human spirit. For example, although people seek therapeutic solutions to troubling issues, Mehl contended that the images of the hero, the saint, and the artist awakened the desire of human beings to meet challenges in life. Despite the efforts to make Beethoven's symphonies into background music, great works of art did not induce tranquility or consumerism. Their original purpose reappeared as they inspired a desire to bring transcendent beauty closer to earth. Mehl thought the greatest danger facing modern society was the arrogance of racism. This was an effort to revile a group for a human quality, such as soul, that resisted the false promises of corporate America (Mehl 1972, 205–13).

MAXINE GREENE: LITERATURE TO BLEND PHILOSOPHY AND HISTORY OF EDUCATION

For Greene, literature offered a historical record people could use to think about the aims of education. In *The Public School and the Private Vision*,

Greene contrasted the ways nineteenth century school people extolled the promise of education with the ways artists warned about the dangers facing Americans. By contrasting the views of educators and imaginative authors, Greene showed how different people focused on different aspects of the reality they shared. For example, during the antebellum period in the United States, common school advocates such as Horace Mann thought about the possibilities of achieving practical goals while imaginative authors such as Herman Melville worried that things might turn out badly. Further, while common school advocates wanted people to know things, imaginative authors wanted people to develop feelings for situations (Greene 1965, 4).

In a similar manner, Greene used literature and history to reveal how philosophical descriptions of social reality changed over time. During the colonial period, the Puritans or the Moravians transmitted their religious views of reality through their schools. As the colonies prospered, the colonists interacted, and the combinations of their perceptions gave way to competing conceptions of values. For example, Benjamin Franklin proposed an academy that served the rising merchant class, and Thomas Jefferson proposed a system of free schools that trained leaders for a representative democracy. Greene set these perspectives opposite each other in a chronological order in ways to reveal the variations that contributed to the development of a social ideal (Greene 1965, 4–8).

In the last chapter of *The Public School and the Private Vision*, Greene praised John Dewey for finding imaginative ways out of crippling dualisms such as the difference between play and work or the separation of mind and body. At the same time, Greene turned to F. Scott Fitzgerald's *The Great Gatsby* to warn educators against the pursuit of simplistic goals. Gatsby's demise came from his tendency to uphold innocent ideals while striving to be with people who pursued vulgar aims. In this way, Greene maintained that educators should define inclusive meanings that could turn people into comrades (Greene 1965, 153–66).

About a decade later, Greene published a collection of essays entitled *Landscapes of Learning*. The title implied that historical changes justified the move to phenomenology from the pragmatism of Dewey. She claimed that Dewey built his ideas on the view popular in the early parts of the twentieth century that scientists constructed their theories by having conversations with other scientists about their interpretations of their experiments.

Unfortunately, Greene found that, by the 1970s, many people lacked faith in intellectual thought and they withdrew from potential controversies. The result was that each individual developed his or her own unique perspective dependent on the landscape their situation revealed. To some extent, scientists fed the problems because scientists suggested techniques to reduce difficulties. According to Greene, the benefit that phenomenology offered was the inspiration to look through the eyes of other people to overcome individualism. She believed a person could become more authentic by being engaged with other people and aware of how they encountered the world (Greene 1978, 8–11).

Greene's concern with phenomenology enabled her to look at programs educators offered to encourage pluralism and tolerance. She warned that affection for pluralism could make democracy difficult because the ideal of community, which was basic to democracy, implied that people should share value orientations. Diversity implied that each group of people had its own set of values and perspectives, and pluralism required that people value tolerance. The contradiction that arose from multiculturalism was the suggestion that people should agree to end discrimination rather than share a positive value.

Despite these dangers, Greene found in phenomenology a defense for pluralism, which she explained in her book *Releasing the Imagination*. Contending that various groups had recently asserted their identity, she considered this as an opportunity to imagine new ways to expand the notion of community by learning about the emotions these individuals felt when they met members of other groups. Greene based her argument on the definition of community as the result of people joining to form something they could share because they could speak from a sense of who they were. She believed that human beings formed a plurality naturally because each person perceived things from his or her perspective. In a similar way, common objects, such as flowers, classrooms, or streets, showed their reality in the combined perceptions of individuals (Greene 1995, 155–57).

To illustrate how pluralism could form community, Greene described how Toni Morrison had pursued her freedom as a writer in a world that discriminated against her. When Morrison illuminated the culture of her group for her readers, she enabled them to see themselves more clearly. This meant that art or school curricula should show the perspectives of many different individuals in ways that revealed the life-affirming qualities that different groups shared and how each group held the quality in a unique way. The problem was that when classroom lessons stressed different practices people followed, the lessons altered what everyone shared. She added that classrooms could be places where children entered into dialogue with each other as caring people and where teachers were concerned for them all (Greene 1995, 158–68).

While Greene realized that freedom was more than the absence of restraint, she explained in *The Dialectic of Freedom* that there were contradictory relations in every human situation. The relationship of two poles standing opposite each other implied that some form of meeting was possible. There may not be a perfect synthesis of these entities, yet the tensions could become part of people's striving toward some sense of completion. The tension Greene wanted to explore in her book was between different conceptions of freedom found in American literature. She developed a view of education on the notion that the self was something continually changing. Accordingly, she defined education as a process of releasing people to improve themselves (Greene 1998, 1–23).

Greene divided *The Dialectic of Freedom* into three main parts, each of which considered literary works written in America during a specific era or by a particular group. For example, chapter 2 showed how American authors, politicians, and educators urged people to fight for freedom against oppression; however, she complained that these authorities could not agree what positive good freedom would bring. For example, she explained how Mark Twain criticized the inhuman force of industrialization by comparing factories to the steamboat that rushed forward overturning Huck's raft. Unfortunately, she added, Twain offered no alternative to modern capitalism (Greene 1998, 24–31).

In chapter 3, Greene described the efforts women made to discover the oppression under which they lived. An example was Sue Miller's book, *The Good Mother*, in which a woman divorced her husband, fell in love with another man, exposed their intimacy to her child, and lost custody of the child when the former husband went to court to convince authorities that his home was more stable. In response, the woman rejected her lover and pulled into herself (Greene 1998, 57–63).

These stories illustrated to Greene the need for a public space in which people could formulate a positive concept of freedom. Unfortunately, people took freedom for granted or they thought of it as the absence of restrictions to personal choice. These disguised the tensions present in a social world wherein some people dominated other people. She criticized educators who equated freedom with autonomy because the view that people should use rational thought to make decisions excluded women who made decisions based on personal relationships. For Greene, the way out of these difficulties was for people to think about freedom as a special characteristic for specific places and as something that could unite people. This meant that teachers should make situations more visible to the students so that they could interpret the world they shared with other people (Greene 1998, 117–20).

CONCLUSION

Bode, Mehl, and Greene blended history and philosophy to reveal the role that schools should play in different social contexts. In this way, these educators fulfilled the aim of the social foundations of education. They illuminated wider perspectives about education.

REFERENCES

Bode, Boyd H. 1921. *Fundamentals of Education*. New York: Macmillan.
———. 1927. *Modern Educational Theories*. New York: Vintage Books.
———. 1929. *Conflicting Psychologies of Learning*. New York: Heath.
———. 1940. *How We Learn*. New York: Heath.
Council for the Social Foundations of Education (CSFE). 2012. *Standards for Academic and Professional Instruction in Foundations of Education, Educational Studies, and Educational Policy Studies*. 3rd ed. http://csfeonline.org/about/csfe-standards/.
Counts, George S. 1934. *The Social Foundations of Education*. New York: Charles Scribner's Sons.
Greene, Maxine. 1965. *The Public School and the Private Vision: A Search for America in Education and Literature*. New York: Random House.
———. 1978. *Landscapes of Learning*. New York: Teachers College Press.
———. 1995. *Releasing the Imagination: Essays on Education, the Arts, and Social Change*. San Francisco: Jossey-Bass.
———. 1998. *The Dialectic of Freedom*. New York: Teachers College Press.
Hofstadter, Richard. 1963. *Anti-intellectualism in American Life*. New York: Knopf.
Mehl, Bernard. 1963. "Education in American History." In *Foundations of Education*, edited by George F. Kneller, 1–42. New York: John Wiley and Sons.
———. 1966. "Review of *The Public School and the Private Vision* by Maxine Greene," *History of Education Quarterly* 6 (3): 104–6. http://www.jstor.org/stable/367625.
———. 1972. *Classical Educational Ideas from Sumeria to America*. Columbus, OH: Merrill.

Chapter Five

History as Critique and Source of Ideology in Education

Tucson's Outlawed Mexican American Studies Program

Thomas M. Falk

In recent years, we have seen a rise in controversies regarding the appropriateness and legality of some history curricula in public secondary schools, none more prominent than the Tucson Unified School District's outlawed Mexican American Studies Program. Essentially a battle over "the story of us," this case illustrates the dual function of historical instruction as both critique and source of ideology.

Five years ago in Arizona, the Tucson Unified School District voted to eliminate its popular Mexican American Studies Program (MASP), following a ruling that it violated a 2010 state law, [HB] 2281, prohibiting the advocacy of "ethnic solidarity instead of the treatment of students as individuals" and the teaching of "resentment toward any race or class of people" (Huppenthal 2015). In accordance with the law, the district removed seven texts from its classrooms, including *Rethinking Columbus: The Next 500 Years* (Bigelow and Peterson 1998), *Chicano! The History of the Mexican Civil Rights Movement* (Rosales and Rosales 1997), Rodolfo Acuña's *Occupied America* (2010), Paulo Freire's *Pedagogy of the Oppressed* ([1968] 2000), and *Critical Race Theory* (2001) by Richard Delgado and Jean Stefancic. Advocates of the MASP, including its former director, Sean Arce (2012), view the law in light of Arizona's broader racial and xenophobic tensions.

This controversy provides a lens through which to analyze ideological dimensions of history. History is ideological insofar as it concerns ontological questions of humanity and worldview. Educators in Tucson have sought to provide their predominantly Latino students with an alternative to traditional accounts that have rendered their past inconsequential. The MASP's revisionist literature succeeds at critiquing ideology by enlarging "the story of us" to include ancient Mesoamerican civilizations.

Nonetheless, this literature also functions as a source of ideology by selectively omitting the preponderance of pre-Columbians whom Eric Wolf has named "the people without history" (Wolf 1997). These nonliterate, non-state-subject peoples left no written records and therefore remain invisible to the historical gaze. Anthropologists of the past century have, however, begun to reveal that these folks, ancestors to us all, abided lifeways strikingly different from our own. Including them into our origin stories can carry us beyond inherited ideological borders, enriching our appreciation of who we are and what kind of world we might still create.

HOW TUCSON'S MEXICAN AMERICAN STUDIES PROGRAM BECAME OUTLAWED

Prior to 2010, educators in Tucson sought to instruct their largely Latino student population in seeing their history from a narrative perspective distinct from those commonly purveyed in U.S. schools. Explicit in the program's curriculum were analyses of class conflict, critiques of U.S. imperialism, white supremacy, and Manifest Destiny (Acuña 2010; Bigelow and Peterson 1998).

Some opponents of the program, including former state superintendent of public instruction and author of [HB] 2281, Tom Horne, admitted to being "shocked by the racist nature of the curriculum" (quoted in Planas 2012). Horne's successor and former state congressman, John Huppenthal (2012), who coauthored the legislation, "found that these classes were promoting ethnic resentment. They were promoting ethnic solidarity in ways that are really intolerable in an educational environment." Rather than imparting critical perspectives on history, Huppenthal argued, MASP teachers were indoctrinating students with a narrow and one-sided version of history that taught them to hate white folks.

In the course of a programmatic review, the superintendent found teachers utilizing Freire's *Pedagogy of the Oppressed* to "put together a Marxian model in which the oppressed are the Hispanic students and the oppressors are the white Caucasian power structure. We came to the conclusion that it wasn't okay to be preaching that model in the classroom." The major point, said Huppenthal (2012), is that we want to "create a society in which everybody is working for a better tomorrow, not working to get even."

MASP supporters argue that the curriculum helps underprivileged students to succeed. Statistical measures have demonstrated higher attendance rates and grades among students enrolled in the program (Cabrera, Milem, and Marx 2012). More significantly, teachers credit the program with motivating formerly disinterested Latino students to consider the power of ideas in their lives. Tucson's current superintendent, H. T. Sanchez, spoke in favor of the "culturally relevant curricula," stating, "It's important for students to see themselves reflected in literature and history. . . . They are more apt to take charge of their own learning and their own education in a powerful way" (quoted in Planas 2015).

Other defenders of the MASP suggest ideological motives behind its ban. According to Arce (2012), the former director, lawmakers have cowed to anti-Mexican and anti-immigrant sentiment in the state: "It is very pervasive, and, unfortunately, it has seeped into our public institutions, particularly our schools, wherein Mexican-American and Latino students are actually dehumanized."

In 2013, a federal court ruled that the district's students should not be prevented from studying culturally relevant material. Claiming that this ruling trumps [HB] 2281, Superintendent Sanchez authorized the MASP's reinstitution (Shaheed 2015). In March of 2015, the new and current superintendent of public instruction, Diane Douglas, announced that the state would not cut funding because the MASP directors had cooperated with requests to monitor the curriculum (Planas 2015).

These are the facts and rhetoric of the case in Tucson, which provide a lens through which to analyze ideological dimensions of history. Such an exercise will cut deeper than issues of race, ethnicity, and nationality. Ultimately, ideological critique of history entails enlarging our conceptions of the human condition and therefore the kind of world we might yet achieve.

HISTORY AS CRITIQUE AND SOURCE OF IDEOLOGY

> Ernest Renan was right when he wrote over a century ago: "Forgetting, and I would even say historical error, are an essential factor in the creation of a nation, and so it is that progress in historical studies is often a danger to nationality." That is, I believe, a fine task for historians: to be a danger to national myths.
> —Eric Hobsbawm (1990, 64)

> There come moments in our lives when certain facts appear before us, startle us, and then cause us to question beliefs that were strongly fixed in our consciousness—embedded there by years of family prejudice, orthodox schooling, imbibing of newspapers, radio, and television. This would seem to lead to a simple conclusion: that we all have an enormous responsibility to bring to the attention of others information they do not have, which has the potential of causing them to rethink long-held ideas.
> —Howard Zinn (2005)

Under proper circumstances, the study of history can disabuse us of falsehoods and illusions. Critical historian Howard Zinn (2004) describes his own experience as revelatory. A decorated WWII pilot who had flown bombing raids over Nazi-occupied Europe, Zinn returned, postwar, to survey the collateral damage. Accounts from the ground revealed that Pentagon reports vastly understated the extent of civilian casualties.

Zinn's experience taught him that there often exists a great gap between official history and the lived experiences of ordinary folk. Thereafter, he dedicated his life's work to illuminating their perspectives, allowing readers to identify with the poor, the rank and file, and the defeated, as much as we have erstwhile identified with the winners and champions of history.

History is more controversial than other academic subjects because of its role in the re-creation of the body social. By telling us where we have been, history casts horizons of where we may go and who we may be when we arrive there. Although the study of historical facts allows us to critique ideology by revealing truth and uncovering myth, history itself appears a sea of ideology that swallows all thinking about who we are and what the world is.

HISTORY AS CRITIQUE OF IDEOLOGY

The controversy in Arizona provides a lens through which to analyze ideological dimensions of history. By offering a historical perspective alternative to those commonly presented in U.S. history textbooks (Loewen 1995), Tucson's Mexican American Studies Program provides its predominantly Latino student population with a more accurate and inspiring portrait of their collective past and present (Martinez 2012). For example, Rodolfo Acuña's *Occupied America* (2010) and *Rethinking Columbus* by Bill Bigelow and Bob Peterson (1998) counter lionizing tales of Christopher Columbus with illustrations of the natives he enslaved and tortured. Through Arturo Rosales and Francisco Rosales's *Chicano! The History of the Mexican Civil Rights Movement* (1997), students examine American history from an ethnic minority perspective, studying ways in which political and economic power structures have oppressed and exploited Chicanos, in addition to the myriad ways in which Chicanos have organized and fought back against these structures.

Central to the MASP cannon, *Occupied America* (Acuña 2010) challenges the traditional rendering of America's cultural genealogy tracing back through the Western Enlightenment, Christian Europe, ancient Rome and Greece, while conspicuously disregarding the lives and contributions of indigenous Americans. In an effort to reassert their history, Acuña begins his text by surveying the ancient Mesoamerican civilizations—Olmec, Maya, Toltec, Tarasco, and Aztec—highlighting their cultural and ethnic connections to modern-day Mexicans: "The mother culture of Mexicans," he writes, "is its indigenous history—a history that has often been disrespected by non-Mexican scholars. Mesoamerican civilizations rival other great civilizations with which they share many features" (1).

Defenders of the MASP point to its effect of boosting self-esteem by teaching students to see themselves as historical agents and inheritors of a rich cultural tradition (Martinez 2012). This provision of pride and confidence in one's sense of self and origin, or lack thereof, is a fundamental ideological function of historical instruction, shaping, for better or worse, young minds' horizons of possibility and purpose (Woodson [1933] 2008).

By highlighting the racial conflicts and class struggles permeating the nation's past and present, the MASP curriculum teaches students to question themes of unity, progress, and providence implicit in traditional accounts. In response, school officials have accused educators of politicizing their classrooms by preaching racism and anti-Americanism. In lieu of these controversial perspectives, school officials in Arizona and elsewhere advocate curricula that "do not promote any particular political position or interpretation of history" (Hartmann 2015).

A hallmark of ideological capture is failure to recognize its existence. The school officials' conceit of believing that one could assume a neutral and objective view of the past betrays a thorough blindness to ideology. Nonetheless, by sharpening our critical lens, we can also spot ideology rooted deeply within the MASP curriculum, of which its purveyors appear unaware.

HISTORY AS SOURCE OF IDEOLOGY

Arising from the unconscious mind, ideology shapes not only our desires but also our worldview and imagination (Wilson 2005). According to Slavoj Žižek (2012), critique of ideology is not simply about overcoming obstacles to realizing our dreams but more significantly about discovering where our dreams come from and then daring to make them bigger.

As George Orwell ([1947] 2008) famously said, "who controls the past, controls the future." The tools of historical vision reveal but a small and peculiar fraction of our human past and therefore limit perceptions of our human nature. However, the previous century of ethnographic research has begun to reveal a great expanse of ontological territory beyond the historical gaze, opening before us new horizons of possibility and purpose.

Here we encounter the ideological error of the MASP literature, which unconsciously reproduces the very worldview with which it seeks to dispense, albeit in a more ethnically diverse hue. While effectively exposing racist and nationalist narratives found in popular U.S. history textbooks, the MASP's revisionist literature misstates facts and in so doing purveys a hegemony of a larger order.

For instance, Acuña (2010) fails to note that the "great civilizations" of the Mexican "mother culture" accounted for only a miniscule portion of the peoples inhabiting the "Mexican" territories at the time of the conquest. By tracing his origin story through the ancient Mesoamerican civilizations, he omits 98 percent of an estimated 100 million preconquest peoples who lived in non-state societies (Chaunu 1964, 117).

Where Acuña (2010) does address non-state societies in territorial Mexico, Texas, and New Mexico, he relegates them to a "peripheral" political presence and primordial stage of societal evolution, implying that they do not merit the same consideration as the Olmec, Toltec, Maya, Tarasco, or Aztec whom they were, he assumes, eschatologically destined to become. This is a bombshell erasure because those non-state-subject peoples, no less the ancestors of modern-day Mexicans, lived in significant contrast to those whom Acuña chooses to remember. By and large living in small, egalitarian, and autonomous assemblages with permeable political boundaries, these societies bore little if any resemblance to the civilizations that, in the MASP curriculum, account for the Mexican origin story (Wolf 1997).

Also prominent among the MASP literature, *Critical Race Theory* (Delgado and Stefancic 2001) acknowledges that *race* and *ethnicity* are primarily social constructions, more political than biological in nature. Nonetheless, by failing to account for political realities in which race and ethnicity may not factor, the authors elevate these terms to ontological categories.

If by race and ethnicity we mean people who identify with shared, distinct ancestral backgrounds and coherent cultural traits, then races and ethnicities appear to reflect the exogenous taxonomies of administrators and anthropologists more so than those of most indigenous people themselves; rarely have those living along the margins of states sat still long enough for their own racial and ethnic portraits. Instead, we observe groups and individuals strategically shifting their identities, histories, and alliances in order to resist the administrative legibility and subsequent state incorporation that such categories facilitate (Scott 2009).

Although intended to displace myth with fact, the history advanced through the MASP literature, no less than traditional narratives, errs by casting the conquest as a clash between civilizations—European American vs. Mexican American—as opposed to a series of encounters between the raw and the cooked, non-state subjects and state subjects, because the facts are that virtually all indigenous peoples resisted what was most commonly for them a sorrowful and dehumanizing passage to becoming "civilized" (Scott 2009).

Herein lies the ideological trope of history. As we study the past in order to better know ourselves, we may in fact undertake a sort of miseducation. Depending existentially upon the written record, history effaces the preponderance of our forebears who left no such records and lived in societies remarkably different from our own.

THE PEOPLE WITHOUT HISTORY

> So accepted now around the world is the idea of the implicit equality and liberty of all people that it is hard to grasp what a profound change in human society it represented. But it is only a little exaggeration to claim that everywhere that liberty is cherished—Britain to Bangladesh, Sweden to Soweto—people are children of the Haudenosaunee and their neighbors. Imagine . . . somehow meeting a member of the Haudenosaunee from 1491. Is it too much to speculate that beneath the swirling tattoos, asymmetrically trimmed hair, and bedizened robes, you would recognize someone much closer to yourself, at least in certain respects, than your own ancestors?
> —Charles Mann (2005, 365)

Popular U.S. history textbooks bear romantic titles such as *Life and Liberty* (Roden et al. 1984), *The Challenge of Freedom* (Sobel et al. 1990), and *Land of Promise* (Berkin and Wood 1983). Despite its achievements in raising critical awareness of the nation's legacy of failure in living up to the ideals captured by those titles, "the story of us" told by Tucson's Mexican American Studies Program asks students to identify with Mesoamerican civilizations whose crimes—mass murder, enslavement, and human sacrifice—shock the conscience no less than those of the conquistadors and imperialists who supplanted them.

Stretching back to the dawn of civilization, the historical gaze reveals a 5,000-year landscape of leviathanic states whose hierarchies and commandment-obedience relations appear to be ubiquitous and inescapable realities of the human condition. This gives students a truncated picture of who they are, where they come from, and what kind of future they may aspire toward.

Beyond the reach of the written record, "the people without history" may offer a more hopeful picture of our human potential. Despite their tremendous diversity, indigenous Americans have been described homogeneously as primitive, non-state-subject peoples inhabiting distinctly egalitarian societies, wherein the authority of leaders did not rely upon the exercise of violent, coercive power (Clastres 1989; Graeber 2004). "Direct field experience, the monographs of researchers, and the oldest chronicles," concludes Pierre Clastres, "leave no room for doubt on this score: if there is something completely alien to an Indian, it is the idea of giving an order or having to obey." (12).

Endless testimonies from colonists and missionaries paint the natives in similar light. "The great and fundamental principles of their policy are," as Robert Rogers (1765, 233) describes the Iroquois to a disbelieving British audience, "that every man is naturally free and independent; that no one on earth . . . has any right to deprive him of his freedom and independency." "Such absolute Notions of Liberty," writes Cadwallader Colden about the Mohawks in 1749, "allow of no Kind of Superiority of one over another, and banish all Servitude from their Territories" (Colden 1922, 100). "Here is nothing so difficult to control as the tribes of America," remarks the Jesuit, Paul le Jeune; "they are born, live, and die in a liberty without restraint; they do not know what is meant by bridle or bit" (1897, 59).

Biologically indistinguishable from you and me, these primitive ancestors were susceptible to the same mortal frailties—ambition, avarice, lust—that plague us today. It appears, however, that they had cultivated, perhaps over the course of hundreds of generations, sophisticated pedagogies for neutralizing those often pestilential aspects of the human condition (Clastres 1989).

Clastres (1989) describes moral-pedagogical worlds of primitive Amerindian societies as safeguards of freedom and autonomy that ensured no individual could fall under the command of another. Among the Guayaki of Paraguay, for instance, reciprocity laws forbade any hunter from eating his own kill, thus placing each in a relation of mutual dependence with all others.

Clastres cites George Catlin's (1832) illustration of Mandan initiation rituals wherein elders inscribed tribal laws, both physically and symbolically, onto initiates' bodies. Stoically enduring hunger, sleeplessness-induced-hallucination, and unspeakable pain over the course of several days, initiates signaled submission to the body social, the lesson being asserted that the life of one was worth no more nor less than the life of any other—and which, Clastres emphasizes, none would ever forget.

Although there were severities and violence to moral pedagogies such as these, and likely to countless others since lost to time, they served perhaps to prevent a greater evil. While primitive warriors undeniably fought and killed, they appear to have done so to far lesser extents and for reasons quite different from soldiers who war on behalf of states.

Whereas the primitive warrior killed to settle blood feuds and to satisfy his own *jouissance*, he did not do so as a means to dominate or enslave. It is uniquely the soldier of the state who has killed upon another's command and for the instrumental purposes of empire (Rubenstein 2012). One could read this to mean, as Perlman (2010) does, that both the *I-It* relation (Buber [1923] 2008) and Hobbes's ([1651] 2009) *war of all against all* may have arisen not in the state of nature but rather with history and the written record.

Historically speaking, writing emerges as an index of the expansionary state: maps of taxable land, debts, contracts, royal decrees, records of property, and conscripts (Clastres 1989; Scott 2009). "Writing," observes Claude Levi-Strauss, "appears to be necessary for the centralized, stratified state to reproduce itself. Writing is a strange thing . . . the one phenomenon which has invariably accompanied it is the formation of cities and empires: the integration into a political system, that is to say, of a considerable number of individuals into a hierarchy of castes and slaves" (Levi-Strauss 1968, 291).

According to both Clastres (1989) and Scott (2009), nonliterate, non-state peoples may have rejected literacy as a means of self-protection, where, within the grasping orbit of states, survival becomes synonymous with state evasion and oral traditions enable folks to more easily shift their genealogies, kinships, and allegiances so as to elude the ruler's power to render them administratively legible and politically subject.

As states are the political units that have left the greatest concentrations of written evidence, their histories have buried over the greater portion of our human past. Fixed in the historical gaze, scholars have, in effect, been relegated to the allegorical Nasruddin, searching for his keys under a streetlamp. "Where did you lose them?" asks a Good Samaritan. "In my house," answers Nasruddin, "but it is dark in there and since there is light out here this is the best place to look" (Ram Dass [1971] 1978, 3:59).

Like Nasruddin, the historical enterprise searches for a human past shrouded in obscurity. By illuminating this dark space, we may bring into view something pedagogically profound: possible selves and worlds lying beyond the historical imagination (Mann 2005; Sahlins 2009; Wolf 1997).

THE ONTOLOGICAL HORIZON

History functions as both critique and source of ideology in education. By exposing racist and nationalist narratives commonly found in U.S. history textbooks, Tucson's Mexican American Studies Program offers students a fuller and more dignifying portrait of their past, present, and future. Nonetheless, the MASP's revisionist texts fall victim to their own ideological trappings, concealing from students the larger portion of their heritage.

Historical instruction purveyed through state schools may be inherently ideological insofar as the creation of state subjects has always been a constitutive purpose of the modern school. All nationalist education systems, whether American, Mexican, or otherwise, teach their young to be the proud children of Leviathan.

Existentially dependent upon the written record, history allows us to see but a small and peculiar fraction of our human past, shining only the faintest light upon our human ancestors who lived in non-state societies, without the tools of writing. Yet history is not the only ground upon which to wage battles over questions of our being.

Philosophical critique of history's role in education compels us to recognize that we are fated to substantial ignorance about our past. Simply appreciating how much we do not and cannot know may liberate us from long-held ideological commitments and in so doing open the imagination to new horizons of possibility and purpose.

Although they left no written records, evidence suggests that the people without history cultivated pedagogies capable of taming the basest aspects of our humanity and faithfully abided, more than any since their time, the ideals of liberty and equality that we today so cherish and struggle to find within ourselves. These ancestors belong not only to the Mexican American and Latino students in Tucson but to all of humanity. By recognizing ourselves in them, and them in ourselves, we might dream more vividly of a different and better world.

REFERENCES

Acuña, Rodolfo. 2010. *Occupied America: A History of Chicanos*. 7th ed. Upper Saddle River, NJ: Pearson Education.

Arce, Sean. 2012. "Arizona Teacher Sean Arce Fired in Latest Crackdown on Acclaimed Mexican American Studies Program." Interviewed by Amy Goodman and Juan Gonzales. Amy Goodman and Juan Gonzalez. April 13. *Democracy Now!* http://www.democracynow.org/2012/4/13/arizona_teacher_sean_arce_fired_in#.

Berkin, Carol, and Leonard Wood. 1983. *Land of Promise*. Glenview, IL: Scott Foresman.

Bigelow, Bill, and Bob Peterson. 1998. *Rethinking Columbus: The Next 500 Years*. 2nd ed. Milwaukee: Rethinking Schools.

Buber, Martin. (1923) 2008. *I and Thou*. Translated by Ronald Smith. London: Continuum.

Cabrera, Nolan, Jeffrey Milem, and Ronald Marx. 2012. "An Empirical Analysis of the Effects of Mexican American Studies Participation on Student Achievement within Tucson Unified School District." University of Arizona College of Education. June 20. https://www.coe.arizona.edu/sites/coe/files/MAS_report_2012_0.pdf.

Caitlin, George. 1832. *Mandan Indian Initiation Ceremony*. Denver Art Museum. http://creativity.denverartmuseum.org/2001_456/.

Chaunu, Pierre. 1964. *L'Amerique et les Amériques*. Paris: A. Colin.

Clastres, Pierre. 1989. *Society against the State*. Translated by Robert Hurley and Abe Stein. New York: Zone Books.

Colden, Cadwallader. 1922. *The History of the Five Indian Nations of Canada Which Are Dependent on the Province of New York*. London: T. Osborne.

Dass, Ram. (1971) 1978. *Be Here Now*. San Cristobal, NM: Lama Foundation.

Delgado, Richard, and Jean Stefancic. 2001. *Critical Race Theory*. New York University Press.

Freire, Paulo. (1968) 2000. *Pedagogy of the Oppressed*. New York: Continuum.

Graeber, David. 2004. *Fragments of an Anarchist Anthropology*. Chicago: Prickly Paradigm.

Hartmann, Margaret. 2015. "Why Oklahoma Lawmakers Voted to Ban AP U.S. History." *New York Magazine*. February 18. http://nymag.com/daily/intelligencer/2015/02/why-oklahoma-lawmakers-want-to-ban-ap-us-history.html.

Hobbes, Thomas. (1651) 2009. *Leviathan*. Project Gutenberg. http://www.gutenberg.org/files/3207/3207.txt.

Hobsbawm, Eric. 1990. *Nations and Nationalism since 1780*. New York: Cambridge University Press.

Huppenthal, John. 2012. "Debating Tucson School District's Book Ban after Suspension of Mexican American Studies Program." Interviewed by Amy Goodman and Nermeen Shaikh. *Democracy Now!* January 18. http://www.democracynow.org/2012/1/18/debating_tucson_school_districts_book_ban.

———. 2015. "Notice of Non-Compliance to H. T. Sanchez." January 2. http://tucson.com/letter-of-noncompliance/pdf_cdd174de-92e9-11e4-9645-6bd77d6e8a88.html.

Le Jeune, Paul. 1897. "Relation of What Occurred in New France in the Year 1637." In *The Jesuit Relations and Allied Documents*. Vol. 12, edited by Reuben Gold Thwaites, 5–268. Cleveland: Burrows.
Levi-Strauss, Claude. 1968. *Tristes Tropiques*. Translated by John Weightman and Doreen Weightman. New York: Anthem.
Loewen, James. 1995. *Lies My Teacher Told Me*. New York: Touchstone.
Mann, Charles. 2005. *1491: New Revelations of the Americas before Columbus*. New York: Knopf.
Martinez, Richard. 2012. "Debating Tucson School District's Book Ban after Suspension of Mexican American Studies Program." Interviewed by Amy Goodman and Nermeen Shaikh. January 18. *Democracy Now!* http://www.democracynow.org/2012/1/18/debating_tucson_school_districts_book_ban.
Orwell, George. (1947) 2008. *1984*. Project Gutenberg. http://gutenberg.net.au/ebooks01/0100021.txt.
Perlman, Fredy. 2010. *Against His-story, Against Leviathan!* Detroit: Black & Red.
Planas, Roque. 2012. "Neither Banned nor Allowed: Mexican American Studies in Limbo in Arizona." *Fox News*. April 19. http://latino.foxnews.com/latino/news/2012/04/19/neither-banned-nor-allowed-mexican-american-studies-in-limbo-in-arizona/.
———. 2015. "Arizona Won't Fine Tucson Schools over Ethnic Studies Courses." *Huffington Post*. March 5. http://www.huffingtonpost.com/2015/03/05/arizona-fine-ethnic-studi_n_6809246.html
Roden, Philip, Robynn Greer, Bruce Kraig, and Betty Bivins. 1984. *Life and Liberty*. Glenview, IL: Scott Foresman.
Rogers, Robert. 1765. *A Concise Account of North America*. London: J. Millan. https://archive.org/details/aconciseaccount00rogeuoft.
Rosales, Arturo, and Francisco Rosales. 1997. *Chicano! A History of the Mexican Civil Rights Movement*. 2nd rev. ed. Houston: Arte Publico.
Rubenstein, Steven. February, 2012. "On the Importance of Visions among the Amazonian Shuar." *Current Anthropology* 53 (1): 39–79.
Sahlins, Marshall. 2009. *The Original Affluent Society*. Seattle: Wormwood.
Scott, James. 2009. *The Art of Not Being Governed*. New Haven, CT: Yale University Press.
Shaheed, Aalia. 2015. "Tucson Schools Go Ahead with Mexican-American Studies, Risking $14 Million in State Funding." *Fox News Latino*. January 9. http://latino.foxnews.com/latino/lifestyle/2015/01/09/tucson-schools-go-ahead-with-mexican-american-studies-risking-14-in-state-funds/.
Sobel, Robert, Roger LaRaus, Linda Ann De Leon, and Harry Morris. 1990. *The Challenge of Freedom*. Mission Hills, CA: Glencoe.
Wilson, Robert Anton. 2005. *Prometheus Rising*. Tempe, AZ: New Falcon.
Wolf, Eric. 1997. *Europe and the People without History*. Berkeley: The University of California Press.
Woodson, Carter. (1933) 2008. *The Mis-Education of the Negro*. [US]: BN Publishing.
Zinn, Howard. 2004. *Howard Zinn: You Can't Be Neutral on a Moving Train* (documentary). Directed by Deb Ellis and Denis Mueller. First Run Features.
———. 2005. "Changing Minds, One at a Time." *Progressive*. March. http://www.progressive.org/march05/zinn0305.php.
Žižek, Slavoj. 2012. *The Pervert's Guide to Ideology* (documentary). Directed by Sophie Fiennes. Zeitgeist Films.

Chapter Six

A Historical Analysis of "Free-Money" Ideology and Ohio State University President George W. Rightmire, 1926–1938

Benjamin A. Johnson

Free-money ideology, articulated and practiced by Harvard president Charles W. Eliot (pres. 1869–1909) and in subsequent decades by the Harvard Endowment Fund Campaign, entailed raising money for unrestricted permanent investments. In other words, unencumbered endowment funds freed up the institution so it need not rely as heavily on tuition or funds raised for overly exclusive purposes, such as restricted funds for buildings or scholarships.

This chapter will discuss the work of Ohio State University president George W. Rightmire (acting pres. 1925–1926; pres. 1926–1938) in light of the developing free-money ideology of his time. It examines whether and how the financial strategies of an educational leader fit the deliberate and explicit emerging free-money ideology of the period. The chapter will also explore the ways in which financial ideology and historical facts, particularly evidence of communications within universities, influence the historical narrative.

THE EMERGENCE OF A "FREE-MONEY" IDEOLOGY

President Eliot developed a free-money ideology that helped Harvard to become the most financially successful university in the country. An important part of Eliot's policy was to spend all income (Kimball and Johnson

2012b). Eliot's 1883 report states, "It is the general purpose of the [Harvard] Corporation to spend every year all their income. They believe that well instructed young men are the best investment or accumulation which the University can make from year to year for the benefit of future generations. As fast as new resources are placed in their hands, whether from increase in the amount of tuition fees, or from the income of new endowments, the [Harvard] Corporation incur new permanent charges" (Eliot 1883, 41–42). In essence, Eliot believed in the investment of financial resources directly into contemporary programs for students. To assure a continuance of funds, Eliot solicited donations to the university's endowment.

Eliot's free-money strategy was later adopted as a preface for the Harvard Endowment Fund Campaign in the late 1910s. As American universities competed among other universities, including foreign universities, "those universities will inevitably win which have the largest amounts of free money" (Harvard Endowment Fund 1919, 8). Eliot claimed, "The only way to increase the amount of such funds is to emphasize the urgent need of them, and then to treat them with such steady consideration that they will have . . . an assured permanence as funds" (Eliot 1907, 58).

Table 6.1. Leading endowments (in thousands of USD) of colleges and universities, 1900–1939

Institution and Year	Harvard University	Columbia University	Yale University	University of Chicago	Stanford University
1900	12,615	13,285	4,942	5,726	18,000
1905	18,036	14,405	7,317	7,752	30,000
1910	21,990	25,846	12,532	14,902	24,000
1915	28,471	30,900	16,153	19,446	23,975
1920	44,569	39,602	24,049	28,364	33,260
1926	76,022	50,389	45,604	35,304	28,394
1930	108,087	73,375	82,857	59,615	27,846
1936	134,600	46,210	95,120	65,390	31,400
1939	141,250	70,714	100,449	70,944	30,503

Eliot's ideology was taking hold just as the money to support it was becoming more readily available. In the early 1900s, incredible growth was seen by scholars and observers in the number and size of charitable foundations and endowments. Eduard Lindeman commented that, through the 1800s, "only five persons of wealth established foundations for philanthropic purposes. . . . Thereafter the trend grew apace. Six new foundations were established during the first decade of the twentieth century, twenty-two during the second, and forty-one in the third" (Lindeman 1936, 18). Henry Pritchett commented that higher education was a particularly popular recipient of funds from such foundations, and from 1900 to 1930, "the great bulk of such endowments [we]re held by the colleges and universities" (1929, 520). With Eliot's ideology in place at Harvard, the university was primed to solicit these funds.

Tables 6.1 through 6.4 show the immense increases in the endowments of some of the top colleges and universities from 1900 to 1939. In table 6.1, we see that Harvard took a significant lead over other private universities at the beginning of the century. In tables 6.2 and 6.3, corresponding information is shown for the public universities with the highest endowments. A similar trend of increase is noted, though on a smaller scale.

Table 6.2. Highest ranked endowment (in thousands of USD) public universities, 1920

University of California	7,254
University of Washington	6,344
University of Minnesota	3,860
University of Oklahoma	3,670

Table 6.3. Highest ranked endowment (in thousands of USD) public universities, 1930

University of Texas	23,960
University of California	15,223
University of Virginia	9,980
University of Minnesota	8,755

The growth of Harvard's endowment was unique, not only in that it quickly eclipsed other universities' endowment values but also for the strategy Harvard employed in the allocation of gifts. Other wealthy universities received much larger gifts than did Harvard. But Harvard, thanks to President Charles W. Eliot, allocated the largest portion of gifts to the permanent endowment. He was the first university president to develop this policy.

Like other university presidents, he assumed that colleges and universities would succeed or fail based on "survival of the fittest" (Kimball and Johnson 2012a; Harper 1905; Veysey 1965; Geiger 1986), but Eliot understood that this survival would be based on increasing the wealth of the university. He argued, "If the primacy of Harvard University among American institutions of education is to be maintained, it must not be surpassed by any other in material resources" (Eliot 1897, 43).

And Eliot knew Harvard was not only competing with other private institutions but also with public. Eliot and other presidents of private universities felt the threat of "formidable competition with a large number of strong State universities in which tuition is free" (Eliot 1908, 16). While universities such as Yale and Princeton divided their gifts among buildings, the endowment, and other costs, Harvard poured its gifts into the endowment (Holt 1917; "Yale Bi-centenary" 1901; Betts 1916; Geiger 1986; "Princeton Opens" 1919).

Eliot's policies were so successful and well liked by the Harvard alumni that, even after Eliot's retirement, his financial policies were continued (Smith 1986) and Harvard's five-year endowment campaign ending in 1921 attracted national attention, especially from other colleges and universities ("Call for Harvard" 1917; "To Raise" 1921; "Universities Ask" 1920; Wadsworth 1919). Before the campaign was even complete, other universities had recognized its success, and by February of 1920, Princeton president Hibben claimed that about seventy-five universities and colleges were hurrying to follow suit (Kimball and Johnson 2012b, 2012a). It seemed apparent that the Harvard Endowment Fund's adoption of Eliot's declaration, that "those universities will inevitably win which have the largest amounts of free money," was influencing other universities (HEF 1919, 8), including the University of Michigan (U-M), a public land-grant university.

While Eliot's free-money ideology was taking root at many universities, there were others that clung to other, often older ideologies about university financing and the roles of the university president. Ohio State University (OSU), another public land-grant university, would not successfully draw on this type of strategy on a large scale until 1938 (Johnson 2013).

"FREE-MONEY" IDEOLOGY AND GEORGE W. RIGHTMIRE

How then, did OSU's policies compare to this emerging ideology of the time? George W. Rightmire was president of Ohio State University during the 1920s and 1930s, and his policies reflect specific values and ideologies (Johnson 2013). Rightmire appeared to operate under a different set of beliefs from Eliot's. Rightmire understood basic tenets of free-money ideology but did not agree with the need to employ that ideology at public universities, so Rightmire was not successful according to the ideology's criteria.

Despite Harvard enjoying the most financial success, it was not to Harvard that Rightmire and OSU looked for an example of fundraising. Because Rightmire and many others at OSU compared their university funding practices to the University of Michigan, the University of Michigan is used as a comparison point for how Eliot's ideology was employed at public land-grant institutions.

President Rightmire's early correspondence and reports reflect his attitudes about private fundraising and his own role in the university's finances, as well as the progress (or lack thereof) in soliciting gifts for the university

(OSU Archives 1926–1938). A number of pieces to the puzzle emerge from these sources.

First, it is very apparent that President Rightmire had little interest in becoming personally involved in soliciting gifts for the university. He claimed his position was that of academic leader whose most important role was to improve education at his school, not to fundraise.

Second, Rightmire trusted the state would continue to provide for all the needs of the university and this despite the rising numbers of students enrolled without proportional rises in the state appropriation. When the university accepted money from private sources, Rightmire wrote that the university was acting as a steward of the gift rather than the beneficiary of the gift. It is evident in his correspondence that Rightmire, along with other university leaders, feared private giving would result in decreased state appropriations.

A third key issue during Rightmire's early years was his inattention to, or delay in acting upon, the persistent advice of the alumni leaders, specifically the Ohio State University Association president and secretary, regarding the active pursuit of private fundraising and the initiation of a development fund. The OSU Association president, James F. Lincoln, and alumni secretary, James L. Morrill, followed by his successor as secretary, John B. Fullen, all repeatedly encouraged Rightmire to engage in private fundraising and especially to make use of the alumni. Rightmire saw the alumni as a tool for pressuring the state to give better appropriations to the university, but the OSU Association leadership saw alumni as potential donors and active participants in private fundraising. Despite their urgent advice, Rightmire delayed making a list of university needs that could be met by private means and avoided involvement with potential donors. Instead, he shunted important decisions to slow-moving committees.

Fourth, sources show that Rightmire was aware of the examples of other universities, such as the University of Michigan, to which he specifically looked for comparison (Johnson 2013). Michigan led successful private fundraising campaigns, but while he applauded their work, Rightmire was not quick to follow their example. His advisors, looking to Michigan, urged Rightmire to hasten fundraising, but he gave them little response.

Instead of concernedly focusing only on the state legislature (as did Rightmire), the University of Michigan turned much of their its and efforts to its alumni. In 1925, OSU alumni secretary James Lewis Morrill put it this way:

> American alumni, since the war, have raised more than $200,000,000 for their colleges and universities. President M. L. Burton of the University of Michigan has said that the *state universities* may look reasonably to the various state legislatures to supply the "necessities" of higher education, but that these universities certainly must look to private givers, their own alumni in particu-

> lar, for the "amenities" of education,—the museums, the funds to encourage liberal research, the finer library endowments, the scholarships, etc. (Morrill 1925, 54)

Michigan administrators saw that if their university was to be great, they needed to solicit outside donations.

Despite repeated failed attempts to convince the legislature to provide adequately, it was not until 1938 that the Ohio State University Development Fund was officially created. It appears the delay was due to Rightmire's failure to see the value of private fundraising and to a lack of consistent impetus from within the university. But as Ohio State dawdled with the idea, universities around the country were putting endowment plans into action, despite the troubled economic times (Fullen 1938). Even in post-Depression years, Rightmire seemed lackluster when it came to fundraising. Though he acknowledged gifts received, Rightmire tended to delay fundraising work.

In the case of Rightmire, a brief outline and discussion of the interplay among facts, narratives, and ideology is in order.

Historical facts related to Rightmire:

- Sources within Rightmire's archived papers include dated correspondence, brochures, pamphlets, annual reports, and photographs (OSU Archives 1926–1938).
- Rightmire comments on leading newspapers, leading alumni, correspondence and brochures related to alumni donations, fundraising, and endowment topics at OSU and U-M.

Interpretation and narrative:

- Rightmire ignored or was slow to listen to advice from his colleagues.
- He shifted fundraising responsibilities to slow-working committees and was indecisive when these committees brought him consensus or results.
- Believed the state should and would provide for the university and that he and OSU would not be obligated to engage in private fundraising.

Based on the facts, interpretation, and narrative, including the financial philosophies of the time, the case of Rightmire's Ohio State University shows that he respected from a distance but did not accept the free-money ideology that remained the strategy of the most forward-thinking and wealthiest universities. Unfortunately, Rightmire's reticence to engage in private fundraising and to grow the endowment set OSU's financial progress back by decades.

If we were to only use a presentist ideology not based on ideology of the period, we may see Rightmire as someone who did not understand the importance of private fundraising and endowment building. This, however, would be an anachronistic perspective. By judging Rightmire based on an emerging and prevailing ideology of the period, we see that he was slow to react in comparison to other university presidents and administrators. We see that because he rejected the tenets of the free-money ideology, he held back the growth of the university's wealth. By using the historical ideology we may broaden the context. When we analyze Rightmire's case study through the ideology that was growing in power at the time, it expands our perspective beyond what we would assign meaning to on our own, using our current ideology.

Consider also the importance of selecting appropriate universities to be used in comparison to Ohio State when looking at the ideologies of the time. The first inclination may be to compare OSU to another university funded by the Morrill Land-Grant Act (1862, 1890). This may not be historically accurate, however. For example, one might consider Michigan State University or Iowa State University as most comparable to OSU, since both are traditional Morrill Land-Grant universities in the Midwest. While University of Michigan *was* technically not a Morrill Land-Grant recipient, its land grant had come earlier from proceeds from the sale of a federal territorial land grant, which could cause some misunderstandings for historians looking back at these universities (Duderstadt 2007).

The most important reason for comparison with U-M rather than any other university, however, is the simple reason that OSU administrators repeatedly compared themselves financially to U-M, a university that purposefully followed Eliot's free-money ideology ("Objectives" 1938). Ohio State administrators compared themselves to U-M, showing who was important to them at the time. Hence, a historical understanding of the then-prevalent ideology and that Michigan was the point of emulation is crucial to understanding the impact and fit of an ideology. If not analyzed in tandem with Eliot's free-money ideology, we might not understand why Rightmire's advisors and committee members compared OSU's endowment to that of U-M.

One pamphlet from 1938 (table 6.4) shows this ideological comparative relationship. In the previous six years, Michigan had "received from her alumni $3,000,000," while Ohio State had received just $85,000. The pamphlet announces its goal of $75,000 and admonishes, "the experience of other universities indicates that we must secure the following contributions." This call for money is followed by detailed figures on the number of contributions and amount type ("Objectives" 1938).

Table 6.4. Contributions by Alumni to Five State Universities (University of Michigan, University of Wisconsin, University of Illinois, University of Minnesota, and The Ohio State University) to 1938 ("Objectives" 1938).

Year or Organization	Name of University	No. of Degrees Conferred	Amount Contributed by Alumni
1817	Michigan	55,360	$25,000,000
1848	Wisconsin	41,229	4,112,691
1868	Illinois	49,275	2,541,000
1851	Minnesota	38,717	2,000,000
1870	Ohio State	44,461	685,037*

* Including $480,000 for the stadium

During the last 6 years:

Michigan received from her alumni $3,000,000

Ohio State received from her alumni $85,000

Yet again, if we did not understand that Michigan's ideology was based on Eliot's and that Rightmire's aministrators compared their financial decisions to that of Michigan's administrators, we might assign very different meaning to Rightmire's financial decisions.

CONCLUSION

Exploring an emerging ideology alongside a historical case study, in this case Charles W. Eliot's "free-money" ideology and Ohio State University, can illustrate the relationship between history and philosophy of education. President Rightmire's financial strategies are understood very differently when compared to those adopted at other universities, particularly those that accepted Eliot's ideology. When used together, history and philosophy inform the analysis, the meaning itself deepens, and the spotlight of the historical inquiry broadens. Eliot's emerging ideology became widely accepted by the 1920s and 1930s. This ideology became more than just a lens. Rather, it developed into a shaping influence in the history and philosophy of education and still affects the way educators and practitioners view university fundraising (Proper and Caboni 2014; Smith-Barrow 2015).

REFERENCES

Betts, Samuel R. 1916. "General Alumni Gifts to Yale." In *The Book of the Yale Pageant, 21 October 1916*, edited by George H. Nettleton. New Haven, CT: Yale University Press.
"Call for Harvard." 1917. *Boston Globe*. January 11, 1–2.

Duderstadt, James J. 2007. *The View from the Helm: Leading the American University during an Era of Change.* Ann Arbor: University of Michigan Press.

Eliot, Charles W. 1883. *Annual Reports of the President and Treasurer of Harvard College, 1882–83.* Cambridge, MA: John Wilson and Son.

———. 1897. *Annual Reports of the President and Treasurer of Harvard College, 1895–96.* Cambridge, MA: John Wilson and Son.

———. 1907. *Annual Reports of the President and Treasurer of Harvard College, 1905–1906.* Cambridge, MA: Harvard University.

———. 1908. *Annual Reports of the President and Treasurer of Harvard College, 1906–1907.* Cambridge, MA: Harvard University.

Fullen, John B. 1938. District Governors' Bulletin. January 21. 3/f Alumni: OSU Association: Letters, Feb. 1935–Jan. 1938.

Geiger, Roger L. 1986. *To Advance Knowledge: The Growth of American Research Universities, 1900–1940.* New York: Oxford University Press.

Harper, William R. 1905. *The Trend in Higher Education.* Chicago: University of Chicago Press.

Harvard Endowment Fund. 1919. *Harvard and the Future.* Cambridge, MA: Harvard University Press.

Holt, George C. 1917. "The Origin of the Yale Alumni Fund." *Yale Alumni Weekly.* February 2. 528–29.

Johnson, Benjamin Ashby. 2013. "Fundraising and Endowment Building at a Land Grant University during the Critical Period, 1910–1940: The Failure of Ohio State." PhD diss., Ohio State University.

Kimball, Bruce A., and Benjamin A. Johnson 2012a. "The Beginning of 'Free Money' Ideology in American Universities: Charles W. Eliot at Harvard, 1869–1909." *History of Education Quarterly* 52 (2): 222–50.

———. 2012b. "The Inception of the Meaning and Significance of Endowment in American Higher Education, 1890–1930." *Teachers College Record* 114 (10): 1–32.

Lindeman, Eduard C. 1936. *Wealth and Culture.* New York: Harcourt Brace.

Morrill, J. L. 1925. [Correspondence to Ohio State Day Speakers]. November 25. 3/f Alumni: Ohio State University Association and Club Matters, 1928–29, box 2, folder 54.

"Objectives of the First Annual Program, The Ohio State University Development Fund: Representing a Coordinated Movement of the Alumni, Former Students and Friends of the Ohio State University to Provide for Its Special Needs." 1938. In "Development Office of University: 1937–1989." Ohio State University Archives Information File. Ohio State University Archives. 1926–1938. George Washington Rightmire Papers (3/f).

"Princeton Opens $14,000,000 Drive." 1919. *New York Times.* September 27, 13.

Pritchett, Henry S. 1929. "The Use and Abuse of Endowments." *Atlantic Monthly.* 144 (October): 520.

Proper, Eve, and Timothy C. Caboni. 2014. *Institutional Advancement: What We Know.* New York: Palgrave Macmillan.

Smith, Richard N. 1986. *The Harvard Century: The Making of a University to a Nation.* Cambridge, MA: Harvard University Press.

Smith-Barrow, Delece. 2015. "Ten Universities with the Largest Endowments." June 10. http://www.usnews.com/education/best-colleges/the-short-list-college/articles/2015/10/06/10-universities-with-the-largest-endowments.

"To Raise Million A Year for Harvard." 1921. *Boston Globe.* June 30, 4.

"Universities Ask over $200,000,000." 1920. *New York Times.* February 8, E1.

U.S. Bureau of Education. 1925. *Biennial Survey of Education 1920–22.* Washington: GPO, 2:384–425.

———. 1928. *Biennial Survey of Education 1924–26.* Washington: GPO, 2:863–945.

———. 1932. *Biennial Survey of Education 1928–1930.* Washington: GPO, 2:480–500.

U.S. Commissioner of Education. 1901. [*Report*] *for the Fiscal Year Ended June 30, 1900.* Washington: GPO, 2:1924–57.

———. 1907. [*Report*] *for the Fiscal Year Ended June 30, 1905.* Washington: GPO, 1:616–35.

———. 1911. *[Report] for the Fiscal Year Ended June 30, 1910.* Washington: GPO, 2:868–942.
———. 1917. *[Report] for the Year Ended June 30, 1916.* Washington: GPO, 2:253–319.
———. 1938. *Biennial Survey of Education . . . 1934–36.* Washington: GPO, 2:256–73.
U.S. Office of Education. 1944. *Statistics of Higher Education, 1939–40 and 1941–42.* Washington: GPO, 2.
Veysey, Laurence R. 1965. *The Emergence of the American University.* Chicago: University of Chicago Press.
Wadsworth, Eliot. 1919. "Campaign Book of the Harvard Endowment Fund Committee." In Thomas W. Lamont, Correspondence 1916–1921, Records of Harvard Endowment Fund, 1916–1939, boxes 1 and 2, Harvard University Archives Correspondence.
"The Yale Bi-centenary Fund." 1901. *New York Times.* June 25, 7.

II

The Need of Philosophical and Historical Study in Educational Knowledge, Policy, and Practice

Chapter Seven

A Modest Plea for Collaborative History and Philosophy of Education

Randall Curren and Charles Dorn

Reflecting on the cramped style of analytical philosophy of education in its early years, the pragmatist philosopher Abraham Edel wrote in 1973 that analytic philosophers of education should integrate "the empirical, the normative, and the contextual (especially the socio-cultural) *within* the analytic method" (Edel 1973, 41). That was good advice, and useful tools for following it were already appearing on the analytic philosopher's workbench.

Normative ethical and political theory was making a comeback, philosophical studies in practical and professional ethics were emerging, and feminist philosophy would soon follow. By the mid-1980s, analytic philosophy had largely overcome the notion that its revolutionary methods made its own past obsolete, and historically informed scholars were busy mining the classics for neglected topics and approaches (Baier 1985; Cooper 1975; Donagan 1985). Some were doing this in ways that engaged "continental" figures and spanned philosophy and literature (Nehamas 1985), philosophy and political-economy (Elster 1985), or philosophy and cognitive science (Haugeland 1985)—the respective figures being Nietzsche, Marx, and Heidegger.

The involvement of philosophers in cognitive science was something of a watershed in legitimating their return to constructive involvement in scientific research, and such involvement has continued in the experimental philosophy movement, philosophy of scientific practice movement, flourishing of moral psychology, and educational psychometrics. Philosophers of education have in recent years collaborated with psychologists and psychometricians (Curren 2004; Norris, Leighton, and Phillips 2004; Ryan, Curren, and Deci 2013), sociologists (Darby and Saatcioglu 2015; Walker, Curren, and Jones 2016), natural scientists (Curren and Metzger 2017), and of course historians

(Ben-Porath and Johanek forthcoming; Curren and Dorn forthcoming; Darby and Rury forthcoming; Dwyer and Peters forthcoming; Justice and MacLeod 2016; Laats and Siegel 2016; Zimmerman and Robertson 2017).

Philosophy of education is a domain of *practical philosophy*, in the twofold sense that its object of study is a domain of human practice and it aspires—often, if not always—to not simply understand, or understand and critique, but to offer guidance for good practice. Such guidance may fall at many points along a spectrum from the very general to the very specific, where "specific" means tailored to the concrete decisions that specific actors must make in actual circumstances. Whatever the level of specificity involved, *action-guiding* philosophy of education must acquire the necessary understanding, identify the relevant action-guiding principles, and bring them together. The kinds of understanding at stake and how they may be acquired is a complicated matter.

Many philosophers have followed Edel's advice to embrace research in other fields as essential sources of understanding in the pursuit of better and more just education. Yet, over the past decade, the experience of bringing philosophers and other educational scholars together at conferences and workshops has suggested that working independently and borrowing from each other's work is a less promising approach than engaging in sustained *collaboration*.

The understanding philosophers must acquire to identify and address specific normative questions about education may not exist and may never exist, because the empirical research may not address all the relevant questions, and the sociologists and historians may not pose those questions at least in part because existing normative inquiries are limited by ignorance of history and social processes. Empirical and normative inquiry must be mutually, recursively informing to overcome this, and it is hard to imagine how such inquiry could occur except though sustained collaboration.

So rather than discuss how historians and philosophers of education can make good use of each other's preexisting work, we will discuss the merits of direct collaboration to produce work that neither historians nor philosophers could produce on their own. We will begin by commenting on the criticisms of "ideal theory," understandings of "non-ideal" theory, and uptake of these ideas in philosophy of education. We will then discuss the rationale and progress of the History and Philosophy of Education Series of historian–philosopher coauthored works, in which we are participating as a series coeditor (Curren) and coauthors. Finally, we will discuss how we have worked together on our own book for this series (Curren and Dorn forthcoming), and what conclusions might be drawn about the respective roles of history and philosophy in guiding educational policy and practice.

ACTION-GUIDING SCHOLARSHIP

The distinction between "ideal" and "non-ideal" theory—meaning normative political theory—has been much discussed in recent years (Bischoff and Shores 2014; Simmons 2010; Stemplowska 2008; Swift 2008). There may be no universally accepted formulation of the distinction, but Rawls's theory of justice (Rawls 1971) has served as a paradigm of ideal theory and target of criticism of ideal theory. Anyone familiar with the theory will know that its focus is fundamental constitutional principles, it assumes full compliance with the principles, it is developed at a high level of abstraction, and it never explicitly mentions such things as racial injustice (though its occupation with the institutional bases of self-respect echo a theme of the civil rights movement).

These characteristics limit the theory's practicality in a number of ways. It is designed to guide the framers of constitutions and is not designed to guide the multitudes of other decision makers whose ethical responsibilities include matters of justice. The prioritizing of its principles of justice is predicated on universal compliance with the principles, making the order of their application problematic in societies that are not fully just. Furthermore, a more practical form of theory would provide actionable guidance in specific non-ideal circumstances—guidance that would not simply provide an account of what would be just but would identify reforms that are feasible and possible to motivate.

Finally, while Rawls holds that consensus psychological, social, political, and natural science can and should be consulted by participants in constitutional and legislative deliberations, he rarely makes use of any such science in addressing specific issues. Practical philosophy took an immense step with *The Theory of Justice*, but its principles of justice are so far removed from workaday decisions about what would be more or less just that not everyone agrees that ideal theory has a useful role to play.

While we think that ideal theory does play important roles, our concern is with "non-ideal theory" and how philosophers of education in particular can contribute to the development and adoption of educational policies and practices that are more just. A simple description of non-ideal theory is that it would be practical in the ways ideal theory is not practical. It would provide specific actors in various positions of authority with justice-enhancing guidance for decisions they can make, and might be persuaded to make, in the non-ideal circumstances in which they must act.

To do this, non-ideal theory must be exquisitely informed about concrete problems of justice, such as the racially disparate impact of ground rules for teacher layoffs (Levinson and Theisen-Homer 2015) or similarly disparate impact of rules for assigning students to schools (Levinson 2015). It must also work as much from the features of the case at hand as from moral and political theory when it identifies relevant normative principles and sorts through their bearing on the case.

Adam Swift writes in an oft-cited paper on non-ideal theory, that:

> It is for the empirical, descriptive/explanatory, social-scientific disciplines to (try to) tell us what states of the world can indeed be realized by what means—with what probabilities, over what time scales—given where we are now. But it is for philosophy to tell us which of those states and means of achieving them are better and worse than one another. On my conception of how things fit together, philosophy provides the careful conceptual and evaluative thinking needed to rank the options that social science tells us to be within the feasible set. Only by bringing the two approaches together can we sensibly judge what to do (Swift 2008, 369; cf. Bischoff and Shores 2014; Brighouse et al. 2016; Schouten and Brighouse 2015).

While accepting this, we feel compelled to point out that there are powerful exercises in what is arguably non-ideal philosophy of education that are a good deal more complicated than this picture conveys—a picture Swift clarifies by saying that the conceptual analysis required of philosophy should yield "precision about the various values at stake" (Swift 2008, 369). This clarifying gloss seems to narrow the role of philosophy to the final steps of a prescriptive inquiry, overlooking the possible roles of conceptual and normative analysis in foundations that must often be laid for those final steps.

Philosophical contributions preliminary to a ranking of feasible options take a variety of forms. They may examine the alleged normative significance of a proposed explanation of an educational phenomenon, such as the hypothesis that the racial achievement gap is attributable to an "oppositional culture" (Lewis 2012), or may provide one aspect of a comparative normative assessment of the possible benefits of a model of educational reform, such as charter schools (Ben-Porath 2012). These and other forms of empirically informed work on matters of educational justice may provide enough of the "careful conceptual and evaluative thinking needed to rank options" for them to qualify as contributions to non-ideal theory as it is defined in the inset quotation from Swift, even if it does not deliver an actionable recommendation. It may be best to think of non-ideal theoretical contributions to improving educational quality and equity as exhibiting a variety of forms.

It is also unclear how the relationship between practical and professional ethics and non-ideal theory should be defined. There are many shades of practical and professional ethical inquiry, more or less top-down and more or less bottom-up, but empirical attunement, specificity of actor and context, and practicality in non-ideal contexts are not uncommon. Not all ethical studies exhibiting these features of non-ideal theory are expressly concerned with justice as an ethical requirement, but many are.

Bryan Warnick's work on the ethics of video surveillance in schools is an example of such work that would be hard to distinguish from paradigm examples of non-ideal educational theory (Warnick 2007). A very different kind of candidate is the framework for an ethic of academic administration that grew out of a 2006 workshop at the Poynter Center for the Study of Ethics and American Institutions, which brought together ethicists and academic leaders at all levels to discuss real-world cases and the contexts in which academic administrators must make decisions (Curren 2008). It does not provide everything that would be needed to rank proposed courses of action, but it is geared for action in predictably recurring non-ideal circumstances, including the contexts of hiring and evaluating administrators.

In general, there would seem to be many ways in which philosophy can engage other disciplines to make significantly practical contributions to improving education and making it more just. This is true because there are many things it is important to understand, and philosophers can make conceptual and normative contributions to larger efforts to acquire the needed understanding. We believe this is true in the sphere of historical inquiry as well as others.

HISTORY AND PHILOSOPHY OF EDUCATION

How is history and philosophy of education (HPE) related to non-ideal education theory, ethical studies in education, and related breeds of empirically informed philosophy of education? We should be careful to say, first, that we do not insist that HPE must be practical in order to be valuable. There may be ways for historians and philosophers of education to work together that yield valuable new understanding but do not share or fulfill the ambitions of practical philosophy or non-ideal education theory. However, the form of HPE we will describe does have action-guiding ambitions and has at least some of the attributes of non-ideal theory.

The project we have undertaken concerns patriotic education and more specifically the history of attempts to teach patriotic citizenship in schools throughout U.S. history, the conceptions of learning and patriotic virtue evident in those attempts, the rationales invoked, the adequacy of those rationales, whether any adequate rationale can be devised for cultivating patriotism in schools, whether a genuinely virtuous form of patriotism is conceivable, what considerations should guide civic education, and what it should look like. The book we have been writing together is for an HPE book series, coedited by one of us (Curren, a philosopher) and historian Jonathan Zimmerman. We will explain the rationale for the book series first and then illustrate those ideas with reference to our own collaboration.

The idea for the series originated with historian Harold Wechsler, who in 2007 proposed a series of short, education-policy focused, historian–philosopher coauthored works, as a way to combine the strengths of two humanistic fields of educational inquiry, effectively demonstrate the importance of these fields to sound education policy, and fulfill the aspirations of policy-minded members of the History of Education Society.[1]

As the series took shape in 2009, these initial ideas were elaborated in greater detail, drawing inspiration from the IMPACT pamphlet series in philosophy of education addressed to UK policy makers and practitioners.[2] Though single-authored and limited to 12,000 to 16,000 words, the IMPACT pamphlets are models of serious engagement with important aspects of educational policy and practice.

The basic idea of the Curren–Zimmerman series is that philosophy and history of education can together provide a more comprehensive understanding of controversial educational matters, and more compelling guidance for educational policy and practice, than either could alone. A further formative idea is that the best way to bring the two fields together is through philosopher–historian collaborations that are sustained long enough to produce a short book focused on a controversial educational issue.

Philosophers can provide conceptual and normative clarity, but they must enlist the aid of other disciplines if they are to offer well-grounded, practical guidance on matters of public concern. Historians, for their part, can provide an understanding of societies and their institutions that may powerfully inform judgments of contemporary practice and assessments of feasibility, but understanding in itself has no implications for what is to be done without reference to guiding values.

Practical philosophy is largely an art of *making explicit* the architecture of value, but philosophers' limited understanding of institutional and human realities may limit their grasp of the relevant conceptual and ethical terrain. Historians, on the other hand, are loath to moralize but hope the narratives they construct will engage and inform the sympathies of readers in a way that will productively inform policy. Their own sympathies and limited facility with ethical analysis may, however, limit the extent to which their research answers the questions most pertinent to determining a defensible course of action.

These counterpart limitations of history and philosophy bearing on public policy can be remedied through sustained collaboration, whereby historian–philosopher pairs mutually inform each other's work on an educational topic. The result would not simply be a more complete argument for a policy position—an argument that brings together descriptive and normative premises, and is more complete in providing expert articulation of the basis of those premises in disciplined normative *analysis* and historical *research*. It would be an argument grounded in expert normative analysis and historical research *that have mutually informed each other* over the course of a sustained collaboration. The synoptic grasp of an issue this provides may approximate the ideal of ethical case analysis in which the features of the case are understood in light of relevant ethical principles, the principles themselves being neither determined ad hoc by the case nor preselected in a way that yields theory-driven blindness to the nuances of the case.

As with other cross-disciplinary collaborations, there is preparatory talk and sharing of drafts and background readings, but the real work of knitting the disciplines together is in the writing. As Eli Lazarus writes aptly in *Nature* in January 2016, "Writing together makes projects real. . . . The exercise closes conceptual distances that conversations leave wide open" (Lazarus 2016, 429). So interdisciplinary workshops should "scrap hours of showcase presentations" and let attendees write, he insists (429).

With the right funding this is possible, and the authors and editors workshops we organized in November 2012, February 2014, and April 2015 divided the time between author presentation of work-in-progress and time for face-to-face collaboration. The second and third of these were read-ahead affairs in which the presentation sessions became opportunities for authors to not just present but also receive comments based on close readings of their drafts and learn from the experience of others engaged in a novel, common enterprise.

Lazarus is also on target when he writes that the debates we have in reworking drafts tend to yield "simpler, clearer writing—to everyone's benefit. . . . You strike your foregone conclusions, hang up your implicit assumptions and begin to build—and rebuild—explanations and arguments from scratch" (429). This is the key to progress in addressing the important matters that languish in the spaces between disciplinary silos.

AN ILLUSTRATIVE CASE STUDY

Our own collaboration, sustained over six years with many interruptions, is illustrative. We both began from the post-9/11 philosophical literature on patriotism in schools, a literature divided on whether it can ever be appropriate to inculcate patriotism in schools but occupied with common themes. The pathologies and hazards of actual patriotism are well-trodden ground: the association of patriotism with suppression of healthy dissent, the hazards of racialized and exclusionary patriotism, manipulations of patriotism that undermine the legitimacy of government, and the corruption of education. While acknowledging these hazards, others have argued that patriotism can play beneficial roles in unifying countries, wedding citizens to just institutions, securing loyalty and willingness to serve, and enabling countries to endure the rigors of war.

Weighing these arguments, our leading thought was that we would argue that schools should not attempt to inculcate patriotism but should engage in education for democratic citizenship that would channel children's independently developing patriotic sentiments in the most civically productive directions. The initial chapter plan was to organize the three history chapters around the academic curriculum, the co-curriculum, and hidden curriculum, with philosophical chapters to follow on the relevant political philosophy, the debates developed in the scholarly literature, and a comprehensive proposal for civic education.

A great deal changed once the historical chapters were drafted and we worked through them together. It became evident that what Dorn had uncovered in the history of attempts to instill patriotism in U.S. schools did not entirely fit the preexisting curricular categories. It also became evident that the entire plan for the philosophical chapters required a major reorganization so that they began by gathering together the historical rationales for teaching patriotism and associated ideas about its nature and acquisition. With some minor reshuffling and back-and-forth revisions, the historical chapters were reshaped around forms of learning that progressed from knowledge and skills, to sentimental attachment to heroes and participation in rituals, to the mobilizing of students for not just symbolic solidarity but also real acts of national service in time of war. Several unexpected developments followed.

First, a progression of levels of education came into view, moving from elementary reading and writing in chapter 1 to high school in chapter 3, and eventually college in chapter 6, with the chapter 6 theme of education for global citizenship through collaborative problem-focused learning picking up the thread of progressive-era ideas of education for cooperative citizenship discussed in chapter 1.

A second unexpected development was that the language of country and land in documentary sources led us to make a great deal of something we had barely thought about before: the land itself as an object of patriotic attachment. These and some related strands of our work led to the introduction of a general theory of just education, related ideas of civic responsibility, civic intelligence, and civic friendship, and an analysis of virtuous patriotism as appropriate responsiveness to the value of all that a country encompasses.

Another strength of our collaboration, consistent with Lazarus's remarks, was the closing of conceptual distances through the process of writing together. In conceiving of the chapter on heroes and rituals, for instance, we had several preliminary conversations about the forms of patriotic ritual into which Americans have infused meaning over time, in particular the Pledge of Allegiance. Coming to relatively easy agreement on the importance of these rituals in the historical practices of civic education, it was only once we began writing about them that differences between our disciplinary approaches revealed themselves.

Dorn proceeded by taking as his central concern the historical enactment of patriotic sentiment through ritual, while Curren adopted a normative approach to patriotic sentiment as it was manifested through ritualistic practices. Not content with the resulting text, we shared drafts, revised each other's work, and frequently conversed—in person, over the phone, and even by text—about our writing. The outcome was a chapter that, we believe, benefits from an authentic weaving together of the threads of historical and philosophical inquiry into the fabric of a more coherent interpretation.

A final benefit resulting from the collaboration was also linked to our disciplinary backgrounds. Historians, in addition to their reluctance to moralize, loathe "presentism" or the interpretation of past events in relation to contemporary values and beliefs. Consequently, although they are content for their work to inform the present, they tend to avoid crafting studies with the explicit intention of asserting contemporary policy implications.

Practical philosophers, on the other hand, conduct analyses that build arguments for ethically defensible policies and practices. Given this difference, we were confronted with a dilemma: should we construct the project around past events with an eye toward the present or use the present to signpost opportunities for research into the past? After struggling with deciding how to begin, we coauthored a brief proposal based on our shared impressions of both the past and present. Entitled "Should Schools Teach Patriotism?," this two-page document provided a gateway into the collaboration, which we used to outline a plan for the historical research from which Curren drew pertinent themes for further analysis.

We believe that the resulting manuscript, *Patriotic Education: Realizing America in a Global Age*, provides an analysis of schools' efforts to educate for patriotism that is far more nuanced and informed than either of us could have produced on our own. Learning from the past while seeking to foster a more just present, we illuminate the relationship between patriotic and civic education in a way that provides guidance not only for parents, teachers, and administrators but also all who value democracy in America today.

ACKNOWLEDGMENTS

We owe Meira Levinson and Gina Schouten thanks for their comments on a penultimate draft.

REFERENCES

Baier, Annette. 1985. *Postures of the Mind: Essays on Mind and Morals*. Minneapolis: University of Minnesota Press.

Ben-Porath, Sigal. 2012. "School Choice and Educational Opportunity: Rationales, Outcomes and Racial Disparities." *Theory and Research in Education* 10 (2): 171–89.

Ben-Porath, Sigal, and Michael Johanek. Forthcoming. *School Choice: Historical and Philosophical Perspectives*. Chicago: University of Chicago Press.

Bischoff, Kendra, and Kenneth Shores. 2014. "The Role of Social Science in Action-Guiding Philosophy: The Case of Educational Equity." *Theory and Research in Education* 12 (2): 131–50.

Brighouse, Harry, Helen F. Ladd, Susanna Loeb, and Adam Swift. 2016. "Educational Goods and Values: A Framework for Decision-Makers." *Theory and Research in Education* 14 (1): 3–25.

Cooper, John. 1975. *Reason and the Human Good in Aristotle*. Cambridge, MA: Harvard University Press.

Curren, Randall. 2004. "Educational Measurement and Knowledge of Other Minds." *Theory and Research in Education* 2 (3): 235–53.

———. 2008. "Cardinal Virtues of Academic Administration," *Theory and Research in Education* 6 (November 2008): 337–63.

Curren, Randall, and Charles Dorn. Forthcoming. *Patriotic Education: Realizing America in a Global Age*. Chicago: University of Chicago Press.

Curren, Randall, and Ellen Metzger. 2017. *Sustainability: The Art of Preserving Opportunity*. Cambridge, MA: MIT Press.

Darby, Derrick, and John R. Rury. Forthcoming. *The Color of Mind: Why the Origins of the Achievement Gap Matter for Justice*. Chicago: University of Chicago Press.

Darby, Derrick, and Argun Saatcioglu. 2015. "Race, Inequality of Opportunity, and School Choice." *Theory and Research in Education* 13 (1): 56–86.

Donagan, Alan. 1985. *Human Ends and Human Actions: An Exploration of St. Thomas's Treatment*. Milwaukee: Marquette University Press.

Dwyer, James, and Shawn Francis Peters. Forthcoming. *Homeschooling: An Historical and Philosophical Analysis*. Chicago: University of Chicago Press.

Edel, Abraham. 1973. "Analytic Philosophy of Education at the Crossroads." In *Educational Judgments*, edited by J. Doyle, 32–57. London: Routledge.

Elster, Jon. 1985. *Making Sense of Marx*. Cambridge: Cambridge University Press.

Haugeland, John. 1985. *Artificial Intelligence: The Very Idea*. Cambridge, MA: MIT Press.

Justice, Benjamin, and Colin MacLeod. 2016. *Have a Little Faith: Religion, Democracy, and the American Public School*. Chicago: University of Chicago Press.

Laats, Adam, and Harvey Siegel. 2016. *Teaching Evolution in a Creation Nation*. Chicago: University of Chicago Press.

Lazarus, Eli. 2016. "Tracked Changes." *Nature* 529 (January): 429.

Levinson, Meira. 2015. "The Ethics of Pandering in Boston Public Schools' School Assignment Plan." *Theory and Research in Education* 13 (1): 38–55.

Levinson, Meira, and Victoria Theisen-Homer. 2015. "No Justice, No Teachers: Theorizing Less-Unjust Teacher Firings in Los Angeles Unified." *Theory and Research in Education* 13 (2): 139–54.

Lewis, Christopher. 2012. "Oppositional Culture and Educational Opportunity." *Theory and Research in Education* 10 (2): 131–54.

Nehamas, Alexander. 1985. *Nietzsche: Life as Literature*. Cambridge, MA: Harvard University Press.

Norris, Stephen P., Jacqueline P. Leighton, and Linda M. Phillips. 2004. "What Is at Stake in Knowing the Content and Capabilities of Children's Minds?" *Theory and Research in Education* 2 (3): 283–307.

Rawls, John. 1971. *A Theory of Justice*. Cambridge, MA: Harvard University Press.

Ryan, Richard, Randall Curren, and Edward Deci. 2013. "What Humans Need: Flourishing in Aristotelian Philosophy and Self-Determination Theory." In *The Best within Us: Positive Psychology Perspectives on Eudaimonia*, edited by A. S. Waterman, 57–75. Washington, DC: American Psychological Association.

Schouten, Gina, and Harry Brighouse. 2015. "The Relationship between Philosophy and Evidence in Education." *Theory and Research in Education* 13 (1): 5–22.

Simmons, A. John. 2010. "Ideal and Nonideal Theory." *Philosophy and Public Affairs* 38 (1): 5–36.

Stemplowska, Zofia. 2008. "What's Ideal about Ideal Theory?" *Social Theory and Practice* 34 (3): 319–40.
Swift, Adam. 2008. "The Value of Philosophy in Nonideal Circumstances." *Social Theory and Practice* 34 (3): 363–88.
Walker, David, Randall Curren, and Chantel Jones. 2016. "Good Friendships among Children: A Theoretical and Empirical Investigation." *Journal for the Theory of Social Behaviour.* DOI: 10.1111/jtsb.12100.
Warnick, Bryan R. 2007. "Surveillance Cameras in Schools: An Ethical Analysis." *Harvard Educational Review* 77 (Fall): 317–43.
Zimmerman, Jonathan, and Emily Robertson. 2017. *The Elusive Ideal: Teaching Controversial Issues in American Public Schools.* Chicago: University of Chicago Press.

NOTES

1. This was proposed to Curren in conversation in October 2007, and planning for the series began in February 2009 in conversations with Wechsler and Jonathan Zimmerman at NYU. The pairing of authors to topics and with each other began in fall 2009 with a presentation by Curren to the HES business meeting and interviews with prospective authors at HES and APA meetings. Proposals for the series and eight initial titles were approved by the University of Chicago Press in late 2010.

2. Works in this series are available at: http://www.philosophy-of-education.org/publications/IMPACT.html.

Chapter Eight

Educational Practice in Pursuit of Justice Requires Historically Informed and Philosophically Rigorous Scholarship

Winston C. Thompson

While a good many disciplinary insights might be valuable to the abiding goals of education, can a compelling case be made for the *necessity* of both history and philosophy in the pursuit of those aims?[1] Moreover, how might history and philosophy assist the educator in practical concerns?

Toward answering this question, this chapter will identify a general account of an overarching aim in education (i.e., the pursuit of a progressive form of justice), in reference to abiding patterns of disadvantage visited upon various groups in (and in reference to) educational contexts and encounters. The chapter argues that the responsible pursuit of the goals of this liberal view of education requires historical and philosophical scholarship that speaks to the potential practical circumstances of educators.[2]

By this view, educational *practice* and *scholarship* have an essential obligation to engage a historical past while simultaneously pursuing the creation of a morally desirable (and adequately defensible) future. Scholarly work in education ought to be appropriately descriptive of the relevant details of our past and present world in order to normatively detail standards for its improvement. The chapter will use the example of an identity group in order to outline the value of historically informed and philosophically rigorous responses to issues of justice in education.

THINKING ABOUT EDUCATIONAL AIMS

That education is understood as a potentially positive force in projects that pursue justice should not be very surprising; one is hard pressed to find persons who would openly declare that education has no obligation to make positive contributions to that which is "morally right." While many would concede that education *can* be (and too often is) a source of injustice, relatively few would assert that this is its essential state. General intuitions about education tend to understand it as working toward some view of justice. As such, this popular perspective yields productive insights into a generally popular account of the aims of education.

While differing accounts of justice might be instructive here—some in more and others in less congruence with general accounts of education—a family of views within the liberal tradition seems a prime candidate for most of the popular contemporary Western perspectives on education.

Liberalism (of its various stripes and persuasions) is commonly understood to prioritize the joint aims of liberty and equality.[3] Though some descriptions of liberalism acknowledge other driving components to its efforts (e.g., a distrust of power or a faith in social progress), these might also be grouped into or seen as arising from the two main categories (Fawcett 2014). As a capacious conceptual category, liberalism might be best understood as "a search for an ethically acceptable order of human progress among civic equals without recourse to undue power" (456).

Given this definition, it seems appropriate to interpret many persons involved with educational practice and policy (hereafter referred to as educators) as aligned with this tradition, locating their aims in some subcategory of liberalism. Stated plainly, "the search for an order of ethical progress among equals without undue power" presents a useful framework within which to understand the rhetoric and activities of some educators. The arguments of the remainder of this chapter will be directed toward those educators within this liberal tradition who endorse the idea that education ought to have some positive impact (relative to liberalism's definitions) in the lives of the persons who undergo or are impacted by its processes.

The educators who occupy this category are not difficult to identify. Their efforts toward their liberal goals are marked by language of, for instance, "empowering students" by ameliorating power imbalances (Garrison 2008). Moreover, some within this group describe their wishes to prepare their students for effective "civic participation" as equals (Levinson 2012). The list surely continues, but in sum, these educators believe they have an obligation to pursue the goals of their liberal project through education. The liberal aims of liberty and equality are often invoked as drivers of these efforts.

Having identified a group of educators motivated by the pursuit of liberal aims, a set of worries emerges relative to the pursuit of their aims. Though this liberal approach to justice pursued through education might seem to straightforwardly identify its aims, it is not clear how one goes about assessing whether a person has made progress relative to the goals of, for example, liberty and equality. In which ways ought education pursue liberty? Are all freedoms similarly valuable, such that any educational experience that results in increased liberties is justified? In which ways ought education contribute to goals of equality? Does equality in some category deserve precedence over equality in another? Is the liberal educator making progress in her search for ethically arranged circumstances of equality and freedom from undue power? On what grounds can these questions be answered?

To some degree, these questions require an assessment of whether particular experiences have resulted in persons and their arrangements proceeding in morally justifiable ways. These questions require an organizational framework in which an observer can appropriately understand and weigh potential outcomes against one another and their various alternatives. This is to ask: in the pursuit of liberal aims, to what types of issues (to say nothing yet of the specific issues themselves) ought one be attentive?

A number of category candidates (i.e., groupings or types of outcomes that might be used) exist for organizing assessments of whether someone is making progress relative to the liberal aims in education. Of these, two deserve special mention, given their scope.

Political Aims

The first is the political category. Liberal educators who attend to this category suggest that, after having had an educational experience, persons ought to have progressed in their political standing relative to their previous circumstances. This political standing includes many domains of life in the polis, that is, life lived among and in reference to others. This category constitutes the lion's share of liberal educators' concerns.

For instance, even a cursory survey of various liberal educational efforts finds reference to their efficacy in assisting persons to better navigate the structures of a democracy (understood as informed voting, engaged participation in the wider community, or any point along this spectrum) (McLaughlin 1995). Furthermore, examples of liberal arguments in education that attend to various economic or social issues of employment, wealth, and socioeconomic class exist in abundance. In these ways, liberal educators justify their activities by reference to their role in rendering persons better off than they previously were, identifying the potential for progress relative to this category of political outcomes.

Pedagogical Aims

The second category contains pedagogical outcomes. Liberal educators who attend to this category suggest that, after having had an educational experience, persons ought to have progressed in their pedagogical standing. This might be articulated as intrinsically valuable as a type of liberty/equality unto itself or instrumentally valuable (with likely reference to political aims). Arguments in this category might suggest, for example, that persons ought to have a fuller understanding of the world, fewer misconceptions and believed falsehoods, or be appropriately prepared for further valuable learning (Mill 1869). Perhaps an increased sense of the value of educational experiences might stand as an additional example of progress in one's pedagogical standing (Dewey 1916). Liberal educators justify their activities by reference to their role in pursuing progress relative to the activity of education itself (which, as mentioned above, may impact the political outcomes of the previous category).

Outfitted with an understanding of potential categories of salience, the liberal educator may begin to inquire into whether her actions under a given set of circumstances contribute to progress in her aims (be they political or pedagogical in the service of her liberal commitments).[4] Successes in these analyses of potential progress will require careful attention to relevant facts, issues, and interpretations. Reference to these categories is insufficient. While it may be helpful to know that one wishes to pursue educational experiences that lead to potential progress in political and/or pedagogical outcomes, holding those categories in mind is merely the first step to productive engagement with these goals. A liberal educator with due attention to these categories can still face authentic dilemmas.

Consider the liberal educator who is dedicated to pursuing progress in the political category but is perplexed by whether those gains ought to be pursued by either (a) ensuring that students are politically literate enough to press for immediate change in a system of one or another (or an overlapping many) pervasive inequalities or (b) ensuring that students are politically prepared for standard forms of participation and success within an admittedly flawed system (Delpit 1995; Hambacher and Thompson 2015).[5]

While the liberal educator might wish to pursue both goals, moments surely exist in which she must prioritize one over the other. With a clear sense of the categories of progress, she would do well to ask herself in these moments: what course of action most likely leads to progress under these circumstances?

To answer this question, one needs to assess potential actions for their ability to achieve progress in the categories of the liberal's overarching project. An organizational framework requires standards for decision making. One needs to have an understanding of (1) the context (including a sense of patterns and abiding concerns) in which these actions are fulfilled, alongside (2) a refined ability to parse and justify motives (so that one can be appropriately confident that one's actions pursue progress). In short: the content and disciplinary tools of history and philosophy are necessary for the liberal educator's pursuit of her aims.

NECESSARY IN PRACTICE

If the liberal educator wishes to pursue progress (as defined by her liberal aims), she needs to know which outcomes qualify as progress and which potential actions get her closer to it. History and philosophy stand as necessary (though not by themselves sufficient) disciplines for the assessment of educational efforts in pursuit of the liberal goals within relevant categories. Together, they grant the educator a clearer view of education itself as it intersects with her aims.

The liberal educator would do well to recognize (and study) the processes of education itself in order to recognize the contexts of her potential actions. In her evaluation of these potential acts, her attempts to determine what constitutes the progress she desires must take into consideration the contextual values and facts of education.

One must draw upon the patterns of meaning and the trends of descriptive and prescriptive priorities to appropriately assess whether an educational experience will "better" a student (or a group of students). If one wishes to do more than stumble blindly toward potential (though not "promised" nor "fully-recognized-when-found") improvements, one must be able to consider the relevant variables and to judiciously compare the legitimating arguments for one course of action over another.

To summarize these points: one needs to attend to the appropriate facts and values of the world (including those relative to the processes of education itself) in one's efforts toward progress. This necessity can be evidenced though the foreign (yet also familiar) example of the liberal educator's experience with quace, as it is, broadly speaking, representative of many similar issues of justice in education.[6]

The Example of Quace

Imagine a liberal educator who has been imported to a world that is not her own. As a newcomer to this world, she knows nothing of the particular features (circumstances, customs, cultures, etc.) of this place. Imagination might be stretched further to accept that she has been given full power in the service of realizing liberal goals in the educational system of this world. The first issue to which she is expected to respond is the reality of quace, a feature of all citizens in this social system.[7]

Unsurprisingly, as someone new to this context, she is rather unsure of what liberal progress might be (or might require) relative to quace and education. In order to act well in pursuit of her aims, she attempts to understand that which she is encountering. Though she is new to this world, she gathers information by reading policy reports regarding quace and education. Unfortunately, each report she reads contains contradicting information such that she remains uncertain of how best to proceed.

The Alpha Report

The Alpha Report states that all persons who live within the boundaries of this society can be categorized by quace. Due to some tradition or bureaucratic vestige (the report is unclear), everyone in this society has a quacial identity. A computer program randomly generates everyone's particular quacial identity, such that a person's quace is unrelated to any fact about her parentage or origin.

In this society, it is not uncommon to have households in which quacial identity differs for all members of a family, regardless of how much siblings physically favor one another or, in their appearance, resemble older generations within the family. A person's quace cannot be ascertained by her physical appearance nor can it be surmised by her linguistic habits or cultural orientation. In this society, a person's quace has no relevance for her future prospects or opportunities. There is no real significance to quace, save as an odd (and antiquated) feature of one's identification documents. It is an inert and arbitrary label, unconnected to educational experiences and entitlements.

The Beta Report

The Beta Report takes issue with descriptions of quace as a nonphysical characteristic disconnected from structures of advantage. Quace, according to the Beta Report, is certainly disconnected from structures of advantage, but it is physically determined. Generally speaking, knowledge of a person's quace is accessible via her appearance. A teacher need only glance at a classroom of students in order to gauge the quacial identities therein. Persons of a particular quacial group share common physical features or (claims of) ancestry but, according to the Beta Report, their quacial identity group membership links them to no discernible pattern of disadvantage or benefit.

The Gamma Report

The Gamma Report asserts a reality that is at odds with the previous two documents. According to the Gamma Report, quace is disconnected from one's origins or appearance. The report claims that quacial identity is random (in this way it is similar to the account in the Alpha Report). Despite this fact, quace is predictably linked to an entire scheme of advantages and obstacles. The Gamma Report claims that public rationales used to justify the practice of prioritizing educational resources operate in alignment with patterns of quacial advantage. Given the weight of these circumstances, most persons have few greater wishes for their child than that their offspring be randomly selected to be a member of one of the better (if not the absolute best) quacial groups.

Discussing the Example

The liberal educator in the quace example is in a difficult position. Which issues in this world are salient? How can she know which educational outcomes move the society closer to her liberal aims? How ought she gain greater confidence in addressing these circumstances in the service of liberty and equality?

Though the example is foreign, its shape might prove familiar when considering one of the many real-world issues that a liberal educator might engage: race. This issue (understood anew, without common assumptions, through the conceptual distance of the quace example) can serve as a token example, a model for engaging other concerns of political or pedagogical circumstance related to education.

A liberal educator requires a sense of history (e.g., the patterns of quacial advantages in the domain of education) and a normative philosophical account of progress in this particular area (e.g., this account might contain sensitivity to the ontological dimensions of quace as it has been and is currently understood) as she pursues the variety of justice defined by the liberal tradition. The quace example suggests the degree to which reliable historical and (normative) philosophical insights are necessary for determining appropriate action regarding the fictional example of quace, but does the real-world issue of race have need of the very same tools?

In a word: yes. How else ought one understand the ways in which race is relevant to the pursuit of liberal aims? Even if one has chosen to focus on a particular category of educational outcomes (e.g., political outcomes or pedagogical outcomes), how can one gain confidence that a particular course of action constitutes liberal progress for a student (or group of students)? In short, how does one come to appropriately engage race, in the pursuit of progress in education?

A liberal educator tasked with acting within a system of education toward racial progress of the sort described above would need to clearly perceive which sort of issues are salient and, through that knowledge, how the contributing factors ought to be engaged in the service of one's stated goal. Failure to do so would derail the entire enterprise; it simply would not do, for example, to organize an "Alpha"-based response to "Gamma"-type circumstances.

Unfortunately, this happens rather easily (and, quite possibly, often). Without a reliable sense of the historical circumstances that have resulted in the present situation, a person happening upon an educational arrangement has little ground for recognizing the racial (or gendered, or class-based, ability-determined, etc.) situation she has encountered. Without the philosophical tools to analyze what she is witnessing and to organize what she ought to do, the liberal educator can scarcely responsibly interpret or intend. In the real world, the historically ignorant and philosophically illiterate liberal educator is at just as much a loss in her pursuit of justice as she is in the quace example.

In Pursuit of Progress

A historically accurate understanding of the patterns of race and a philosophically rich account of the concept of race is necessary for appropriately productive efforts in pursuit of progress. The example of quace (and the serious potential for misreading and poorly responding to it) in the previous section suggests the existence of a potential type of shortsightedness in liberal responses to the real-world issue of race and education. Just as one would be foolish to respond to the wrong assessment of quace, one would be foolish to misread racial realities that affect educational outcomes. Such misreading (in regard to race or any other categories of interest) undermines the possibility of achieving the liberal aims of progress in educational outcomes.

Assuming that many of the liberal educators who pursue goals of racial progress in education (i.e., better outcomes for those who experience racial disadvantage) are acting in good faith, the fact of the present state of undesirable racialized educational outcomes may be a source of bewilderment (Guinier 2004). Rather than suggest that educators and policy makers have no interest in the liberal project of pursuing progress, these efforts might be understood as stymied by inattention to the historical details of race and the philosophical care in understanding the concept and what progress relative to that concept and reality requires.[8]

Without stable sources of guidance, liberal educators might easily find themselves responding to the real-world issues of race in education with the same (or greater) degree of guesswork as the ill-prepared educator in the quace example. While it is true that some selected responses or strategies would realize success on the subject of race in education, there is precious little certainty in such efforts. Without due guidance, one's victories in realizing expected political or pedagogical outcomes are little more than fortuitous accidents, tantamount to flipping a coin. Even if a liberal educator in these circumstances has a success rate higher than 50 percent in attaining stated outcomes, the chances that these iterate toward the ultimate justice aims of liberalism is a matter of happenstance.

In short, the pursuit of liberal aims is confounded, as unprepared educators have no due basis for any confidence that they possess a sufficiently detailed image of the problems they are attempting to address. Mistaking the formidable and complex issues of, for instance, race and education as though they might be well addressed by a figurative newcomer to the many facts and values of this world is folly. Without a sufficiently clear sense of her circumstances, the liberal adherent risks one or both of two ends:

1. she remains unsure of what *counts* as progress in the political and pedagogical categories, or
2. she remains unsure of what *contributes* to progress in the political and pedagogical categories of liberalism's justice aims.

Of course, both outcomes are undesirable as either corrupts the integrity of the liberal project in educational efforts. The liberal educator needs historical and philosophical tools to guide her practical action. As such, it is necessary for educational scholars to pursue work that erodes these uncertainties and prepares her (and her ilk) to confidently pursue the liberal aims of justice in education.

NECESSARY IN SCHOLARSHIP

Educational scholarship ought to contribute to an educator's appreciation of what counts as and contributes to progress in her goals (be they liberal or otherwise). This is not to imply that all good educational scholarship will result in obvious guidance in practical action. To the contrary, educational scholarship might highlight the complexities of a phenomenon, potentially giving an educator additional notes of pause as she proceeds. Even so, when done well, that work allows the educator to better appreciate the situations she faces and thereby take a greater degree of responsibility for her acts. In many circumstances, introducing this complexity slows action because it disrupts the educator's overconfidence in her understanding of the problems she faces.[9]

Though not by themselves sufficient for realizing educational scholarship's obligations to present educators with appropriate reason for action, history and philosophy stand to offer unique and indispensible contributions to that project.

In the case of the liberal educator's aims, history assists efforts to pursue progress, as the discipline offers insight into the patterns of a particular set of phenomena. In the example of race, pursuit of progress requires awareness of the ways in which racialized groups have been treated and mistreated relative to the outcome categories under consideration. Detailing the history of mis-educational (pedagogic) and disenfranchising (political) outcomes, historical educational scholarship on race equips educators with a sense of the significance of their potential actions against the background of these enduring patterns.

Philosophy assists efforts to pursue progress, as the discipline offers insight into thinking clearly, with normative confidence, about the concepts that delimit a particular set of phenomena. In the example of race, pursuit of the liberal's definition of progress requires an awareness of the ways in which race can be invoked as a concept, the way in which that idea reveals or disguises certain elements of the social world. Additionally, educational scholarship might also engage the history of the philosophical understandings of salient concepts, studying the ways in which the logic of a phenomenon shifts, as these shifts potentially reveal key elements of its structures and potential trajectories. In the service of the liberal educator, this disciplinary orientation allows those who wield it well to consider (and justify) which outcomes constitute and contribute to progress toward justice.

To the extent that educational scholarship can assist educators in understanding their circumstances and aims, it has an obligation to do so. History and philosophy are necessary aspects of the educator's appropriate assessment of what she ought to do. As such, educational scholarship must necessarily engage history and philosophy.[10]

If educational scholarship neglects this obligation, it may contribute to either misguided policy or destructive educational practice. The category of "misguided policy" includes the instances of discordance between rationales and aims, but it is also inclusive of instances of accidental coherence between these rationales and aims (i.e., either choosing the right actions for the wrong reasons or stumbling upon the right reasons by inappropriate methods). Normative philosophical scholarship in education is well poised to address both shortcomings. Of course, while "destructive educational practice" might be anticipated through some analytic analyses, the historical perspective on patterns of injustice cautions against practices that perpetuate those patterns.

CONCLUSION

In the preceding sections, this chapter argues that it is necessary for educators and scholars who seek to realize justice aims to engage both history and philosophy in those efforts. One popular account of justice aims in education, the capacious liberal account, is offered, and the organizing categories of its potential outcomes are discussed. While these outcome categories are helpful in thinking about an educator's aim (namely, liberal progress toward justice), they do not, by themselves, provide good cause for selecting a course of action.

The hypothetical example of quace highlights the types of information an educator needs in order to select a course of action that pursues her aim of liberal progress. This hypothetical example sharpens attention to features of the real-world example of race (which might be representative of any number of issues salient to the liberal educator's sense of justice). The pursuit of liberal progress is shown to require historical sensitivity and normative conceptual clarity. Via its duty to contribute to the decision-making processes of educators, educational scholarship cannot escape engaging history and philosophy. These two disciplines are necessary for the liberal educator's responsible efforts toward justice. One might imagine this necessity to similarly extend across other traditions and accounts of justice.

REFERENCES

Delpit, Lisa. 1995. *Other People's Children: Cultural Conflict in the Classroom*. New York: New Press.
Dewey, John. 1916. *Democracy and Education*. New York: Free Press.
Fawcett, Edmund. 2014. *Liberalism: The Life of an Idea*. Princeton: Princeton University Press.
Garrison, William. 2008. "Democracy and Education: Empowering Students to Make Sense of Their World." *Phi Beta Kappan* 89:347–48.
Guinier, Lani. 2004. "From Racial Liberalism to Racial Literacy: *Brown v. Board of Education* and the Interest-Divergence Dilemma." *Journal of American History* 91 (1): 92–118.
Hambacher, Elyse, and Winston C. Thompson. 2015. "Breaking the Mold: Thinking beyond Deficits." *Journal of Educational Controversy* 9 (1): 7.
Levinson, Meira. 2012. *No Citizen Left Behind*. Cambridge, MA: Harvard University Press.
McLaughlin, Terence. 1995. "Liberalism, Education and the Common School." *Journal of Philosophy and Education* 29 (2): 239–55.
Mill, John Stuart. 1869. *On Liberty*. Oxford: Oxford University Press.
Mills, Charles W. 1998. *Blackness Visible: Essays on Philosophy and Race*. Cornell: Cornell University Press.

NOTES

1. This chapter argues for necessity rather than sufficiency. Though not discussed within these pages, potential sufficiency arguments seem rather unattractive as they narrow the scope of educational scholarship (and practice).

2. Rather than assume an audience already loyal to these disciplines, this argument will be presented in broad form to an audience interested in, but not yet committed to, the conclusions of the chapter. Additionally, given its objectives, this chapter will not present especially intricate arguments about the nature of historical or philosophical scholarship. For the purposes of this chapter, both disciplines can be understood by their most general characteristics, though this chapter may invoke constitutive characteristic as necessary.

3. While there are a number of ways in which to understand liberalism, due to issues of space, these are not detailed here. The general version used in the chapter ought to capture most subcategories of the tradition.

4. This chapter presents two example categories of a potential multitude.

5. A pedagogical dilemma may analogously contain uncertainties about whether a particular lesson is justified or ambiguity regarding the comparative value of particular educational outcomes—especially under circumstances of finite resources.

6. This example highlights how a liberal educator might grapple with any number of similarly salient issues (ability, gender, socioeconomic class, etc.). By using a foreign concept as a stand-in for race, the nuances of ascertaining the criteria of "progress" and its impact upon educational outcomes in the United States of America may be more sharply seen, without the conceptual baggage of undesired assumptions.

7. The term "quace" is borrowed from philosopher Charles Mills (1998, 42–44). While, my usage of the term differs in minor ways from Mills's own, these differences do not impact the core arguments of this chapter.

8. The case may be made either upon grounds that they are illiberal or that liberalism requires other aims be prioritized.

9. For example, many educators think they have a firm grasp on race and, as such, an almost reflexive sense of how to address it well. This chapter's quace example illustrates how educational scholarship can provide some distance from seemingly settled issues, such that the complexities of the circumstances are more fully appreciated.

10. As a portion of that engagement, educational scholarship should also provide insights into the educator's decision-making processes. For example, this includes delineating what might be meant by "appropriateness" or "sufficiency" in empirical and analytical clarity relative to educational decision making.

Chapter Nine

The Predicament of Culture and Educational History and Philosophy as Reconciliation

Seeking out the "Disappeared" through Transdisciplinary Engagement

Antoinette Errante

At the 1999 American Educational Research Association meetings in Montreal, I attended a still memorable plenary session on the future of educational historiography. One of the U.S. historians on the distinguished panel bemoaned that "nothing new" had been written in decades and that the scholarship on the educational histories of women and people of color had simply "filled in the blanks." While challenging this portrayal of recent scholarship, an audience member asked why, given the inclusion of scholars representing English and French Canadian historical traditions on the panel, there were no Native historians. The French Canadian scholar responded, "Oh, I don't think they have written any books."

I know I was not the only one who left the session troubled by the U.S. scholar's characterization of the field (see, for example, Donato and Lazerson 2000) or to the reduction of historians to those who write books. Still, the field's sense of who is capable of generating innovation and our beliefs in the power of published texts continue to vex our perspectives on what history is, who makes it, and whose version of it gets to be called "history."

Philosophers appear to be struggling with similar challenges. Historians of philosophy and philosophers of history argue about what constitutes evidence and whether history is fact or history is a linguistic turn or history is a linguistic turn that ends up committing the same errors as history as fact

(Goldman 2015; Oyedola 2015; Scott 1993; Stone-Mediatore 1998); whether we are metaphysical or post-metaphysical (Kim 2014); whether philosophy is universal but some cultures have not yet matured into philosophy (Tartaglia 2014); universal and rational and a product of culture (Eze 2001); and how we can have a more or less certain understanding of history and philosophy, even when history or philosophy are understood as contingent and contextual (Dussel 1996; Martinez 2014).

While these debates enliven scholarly discourse, they have also become the criteria by which to judge whether "others" actually "have" histories and philosophies due to "the power to include and exclude" these suggest exchanges since "the claim that something is not *real philosophy* differs crucially from the claim that it is *bad philosophy*. The latter requires engagement, argument, and justification; the former is a way of evading those efforts" (Perkins 2016, 62). The same could be said of history.

Martinez (2014) argues that the disciplinary practice of evasion comes from the scholarly community ignoring "the immediacy of its own practice," resulting in "questions and interests that are typically not recognized within the discipline . . . [being] dismissed and sometimes taken as signs of incompetence (224)." Such evasion risks erasure of perspectives that do not fit into existing academic discursive practices, including "official" discursive practices concerning other people's discursive practices, even when these are meant to be liberatory.

As a Euro-American comparativist and historian of education whose work has focused on the history of educational processes in colonial, post-independence, and post-conflict transitions in South Africa and Mozambique, I have struggled to find room at the academic inn for the perspectives of the Mozambicans and South Africans who have shared with me their life histories and perspectives. They get lost in tensions between scholars who want to reduce these stories to "either empirical evidence or to mere rhetorical constructions" (Stone-Mediatore 1998, 130–31). Surely, some colleagues ask, I do not mean to suggest a traditional healer's perspectives on history and trauma should be evaluated with the same regard as those of a university professor or that an eighty-year-old man's recollections of his school days could be as valuable a primary source as archival documents.

Since their perspectives are embedded in everyday realities, some of my colleagues do not envision Mozambicans' narratives as having something to teach us per se. Rather than seeing their explanations of why the historical categories of change familiar to Western historians were not relevant to them as a possible critique of those categories, some insist they suggest ignorance or false consciousness regarding the ways their perspectives are constituted by those categories. When Mozambican women's historical imaginaries revolve around shifts in important intimate relationships rather than regime changes that changed nothing for them, some colleagues wonder whether this is ethnography rather than history or whether their perspectives have anything to do with education since the learning contexts they identify as most salient have little to do with formal schooling.

When in the course of telling me about their lives, Mozambicans reflect upon how their lives intersected with broader causes and effects, when they take the time to explain to me their understanding of why things were or are the way they were/are, in my view, they are theorizing. But I am told if I try to engage their theoretical perspectives as theories worth taking seriously, I am merely assuming the position of a scribe. Instead, I am encouraged to theorize in terms dictated by the handful of European scholars who are the darlings du jour of the academic fields I traverse. While these theorists' perspectives are helpful in some instances; in others, they drown out what my participants know and how they know it.

It is not that I am unfamiliar with the complex nature of telling and remembering, and representation, nor do I mean to suggest that these critiques are unimportant. What is evaded, however, is that these scholarly critiques are also discursive practices embedded in contextual and contingent assumptions (Yancy 2015). What is lost when, through our own discursive practices, we theoretically ruminate some voices into silence and erasure?

I do not always feel up to the task of making sense of what I am told with my Western tools and assumptions. No one seems to understand this more than the Mozambicans I have interviewed who explain things that they feel need explaining before I even ask. They will say things like, "Let me tell you what it's like . . ." or, "You see you have to understand that here it is like so . . ."

I have come to understand this kind of perspective taking as an integral part of the experiences that I am trying to understand. Mozambicans' narratives convey not only distinctions between how people see themselves and how others see them but also their perceptions that my understanding of power and resistance is not the same as theirs. They evoke ways of seeing and speaking that come from inhabiting the borderlands and cultivating the sense of double consciousness of which Anzaldúa (1987) and Du Bois (1897) respectively spoke. By contrast, members of dominant groups in any situation "can . . . take their inter-subjective position for granted and thereby make their own sense of the world into a total world, even while making claims to the contrary" (Martinez 2014, 229).

Mozambicans' invitation to show me what lies behind the veil of my Euro-American assumptions is, as Yancy (2015) notes, a "gift" of insight into the myopic nature of the historical understanding I mistook for universal. It is a reminder of what we gain by being more diverse as academic communities and entertaining more self-awareness about how others might think about the way we think and talk about them, an orientation to our scholarly practice that might be fruitful even if it entailed an imaginary dialogue with people long dead.

In the rest of this essay, I explore how these tensions regarding what constitutes history and philosophy reflect what James Clifford (1988) calls the "predicament of culture" and how some historians and philosophers are attempting to rattle the complacent certainties in our practices by taking the notion of cultural practice seriously. After an overview of the meaning of the predicament of culture for our disciplines, I explore how historicizing philosophy and philosophizing history with culture in mind enables us to seek out those that our prevailing philosophical and historical practices have "disappeared." Such transdisciplinary work requires we be open to the reconceptualization of our scholarly practices and discourses that such engagement will likely bring. Utilizing Lugones's (2006) concept of "complex communication," I suggest how imagining this undertaking as a process of reconciliation can provide some guidance to our work.

THE PREDICAMENT OF CULTURE AND EDUCATIONAL HISTORY AND PHILOSOPHY AS CULTURAL PRACTICES

Cultural practices refer to the actions, values, behaviors, and dispositions through which we make sense of and give expression to our world (Bourdieu 1977). They derive their meanings from a group's shared normative framework or "world of meaning" (Avruch 2006). "Culture," does not refer to geographic boundaries but all of the contexts where a group shares a normative framework that informs how they make sense of and give expression to their experiences. Cultural practices embody a group's theory of change and are the vehicles through which power is interpreted, given expression, resisted, and transformed (Comaroff and Comaroff 1992; Dirks, Eley, and Ortner 1994).

We seem to believe certain normative frameworks and practices are better "carriers" of change than others. James Clifford (1988) characterizes this selective appreciation for culture's transformative potential as the "predicament of culture." "Whenever marginal peoples come into a historical or ethnographic space that has been defined by the Western imagination, . . . their distinct histories quickly vanish. What is different about them remains tied to traditional pasts, inherited structures that either resist or yield to the new but cannot produce it" (5).

The "history of emergent differences" thus becomes a history of the universalization of Western practice (Clifford 1988, 17). Our historical and philosophical imaginaries remain saturated with the conceptual binaries the "Western imagination" has created over the last three hundred years: modern/traditional, advanced/backward, literate/illiterate, rational/irrational, scientific/superstitious, and so on.

In order to liberate ourselves from these binaries and tropes, historians and anthropologists like Jean and John Comaroff suggest we rethink our orientation to cultural practices by historicizing anthropology and anthropologizing history (Comaroff and Comaroff 1992; see Dirks, Eley, and Ortner 1994). By approaching history as the change of cultural practices over time, historians gain a more robust lens through which to understand how people change cultures, cultures change people, and both change institutions and societies (Fleury and Garrison 2014). Since P/philosophy is the source of any community's imagination, historicizing philosophy and philosophizing history with cultural practice in mind is a crucial dimension of this endeavor.

HISTORICIZING PHILOSOPHY AS A CULTURAL PRACTICE: THEORIZING HUMAN VARIATION WITH THE PHILOSOPHER'S STONE

To the extent historicizing philosophy recovers dimensions of the work of the discipline as a cultural practice, it is necessarily what Lucius Outlaw calls "a deconstructive challenge . . . [that] decenters the concept of philosophy and its discursive practices into the history of their construction and maintenance . . . and the cultural agenda of the voices in which they became embodied." (Outlaw 1996, 65; see Burch and Sutherland 2006; Mills 2002; Terry 1991). As an example of this, I would like to focus on aspects of the historical elaboration of philosophical theories of race and human variation as these continue to reverberate in our assumptions about intelligence and the criteria by which we police disciplines and their discursive practices.

Modern theories of human variation originate in late German Enlightenment thought that linked discourses concerning slavery with elaborations of the nature of philosophical and historical production and what it meant to be human. Bettina Brandt and Daniel Purdy argue the connection between "the discourse around slavery with late Enlightenment German thought . . . suffers under the double burden of being both controversial and ignored" (2016, 10). This may be because historical scrutiny of the treatment of race by Enlightenment (and post-Enlightenment) philosophers reveals their failure to meet the very criteria of systematic, rational argumentation by which they excluded other philosophical traditions.

I examine three scholarly practices that interrupt the cultural binaries upon which the exclusivity of Western philosophy are based: (1) the dubious sources and not-so-transcendental grounding of early philosophical theories of race; (2) the ways in which philosophical justifications for excluding non-Western philosophy were preceded by redefinitions of the nature of philosophy and history; and (3) the intellectual gymnastics through which non-Western traditions continue to be excluded, even by one of the Enlightenment's great critics, Richard Rorty.

Emmanuel Eze argues that Kant "offer[s] the strongest, if not the only, sufficiently articulated theoretical philosophical justification of the superior/inferior classification of 'races of men' of any European writer up to his time" (Eze 1997, 129). Kant accounts for variation in races on their ability to elevate their humanity through reason, an ability he argues was bestowed by nature in different amounts to different races, with whites/Europeans having the superior ability. Eze notes that Kant's idea of "race" is "not only transcendentally hypostatized but also biologically essentialized" (Eze 1997, 125).

Where did Kant's knowledge of the various characteristics that he attributes to races come from given that he never left Konigsberg? Like most philosophers of his day, he relied on travel journals and reports of explorers, missionaries, and colonizers whose narratives justified Europe's imperialist and civilizing ambitions (Demel 2016). Kant's professional philosophical practices relied less on systematic method and more on the alchemical transmutation of hundreds of missionary and merchants narratives about their experiences abroad into the philosopher's stone that legitimized the construction of universal distinctions between human beings. In so doing, he employed the very kind of magical thinking that he used to justify enslaving Africans as nonhuman.

In their transmutations of travel journals and missionary narratives, Enlightenment scholars went one step further by embellishing those accounts. Hegel, for example, exaggerated narratives of violence in travel and missionary accounts of the Chinese and Africans in order to shore up his arguments that Europe, as the supreme manifestation of spirit, had both history and philosophy, China had history but no philosophy (Bernasconi 2016; Perkins 2016), and "Africa proper" (sub-Saharan Africa) had neither (Bernasconi 2003; Haymes 2008; Kuykendall 1993).

That these were conscious moves can be seen from the fact that Hegel had long thought China at least had philosophy (Bernasconi 2003; Haymes 2008). Until the late eighteenth century, most European philosophers accepted that philosophy existed in cultures beyond Europe. In his 1825 and 1826 lectures on the history of philosophy, Hegel breaks with the prevailing Greco-Roman conceptions of philosophy as a way of life to define it as a scientific system. He then uses this new definition of philosophy to exclude non-Europeans (Bernasconi 2016; Perkins 2016).

While the manner in which philosophy has come to exclude certain non-Western traditions is "peculiarly modern" (Perkins 2016, 74), it is not limited to Enlightenment philosophers. Richard Rorty, though critical of the Enlightenment and Kant, continued to exclude or marginalize non-Western philosophical traditions. Rorty believed philosophy to be the historically contingent result of uniquely European responses to the tension between religion and science. The trouble with the idea of non-Western philosophy for Rorty, Tartaglia (2014) argues, is that it "presents the most glaring counterexample possible to a thesis . . . of the cultural specificity of philosophy. To defend this thesis required him to reject any extension of the philosophical 'conversation' beyond the Western world, despite the fact that this rejection was at odds with many other aspects of his thinking" (1020). Rorty chooses commitment to his historical account for the rise and purpose of philosophy over entertaining the possibility that other cultures might also have equally historically contingent philosophical traditions.

Rorty softens this position in his later years in ways that seem to signal greater appreciation for intercultural dialogue. Still, he remains firm that "the vocabulary of 'twentieth-century Western social democratic intellectuals' may well be the best anybody has yet come up with" (Balslev 1991, 53).

Intercultural engagement in which only one party gets to define the forms, goals, and topics only serves to reproduce the predicament of culture. Indeed, what African American philosophers George Yancy (2015) and Charles Mills (1998, 2002) describe as "the Cartesian predicament" in philosophy is largely a predicament of culture that "places under erasure precisely the philosophical lens through which Black life can be understood, especially within the context of its lived racist trauma" (Yancy 2015, 1147). Yancy reminds us that erasure is not only achieved by disappearing philosophical actors but also by privileging certain philosophical methods and concerns.

> To withdraw from the senses in the style of Descartes . . . is to presume an abstract subject from nowhere. . . .This move actually renders the self incapable of knowing itself, as self-understanding is always already from a here, a place of lived embodied knowledge. . . . Hence, to understand Black lived experience, and to understand African-American philosophy, it is important to begin with embodiment, history, and lived social context, a context within which Black people were/are reduced to an epidermal logic that signifies pure externality, thus denying any subjective interiority to the Black body. (Yancy 2015, 1148)

To the extent that such philosophical frameworks and scholarly practices have shaped and given shape to Western notions of human variation, they have influenced the practice of historical scholarship as well. By virtue of privileging a disembodied individualized self "lost in thought," they gave us a template for normalizing who had history and who had culture, the criteria by which certain ways of speaking and doing could be classified as more or less advanced historical practices, and the groups and moments important to consider in our historical narratives. These cognitions etched a groove in our historical cognitions regarding what it means to be an educated person so that we rarely question the school's centrality as a learning and socialization context.

The point, as Robert Bernasconi (2003) puts it, is not so much the racism of scholars of the past but ours. I would add sexism and ableism as well, for the same practices and processes that have disappeared people of color, also exclude women, LGBTQ persons, and individuals with disabilities as makers of history and thinkers of thoughts (Burch and Sutherland 2006; Stone-Mediatore 1998; Terry 1991).

As a community of philosophers and historians of education, we have an opportunity to bring about a shift in perception about our work by taking seriously those whom our practices have rendered/render invisible. But what does this mean for our work as historians?

SEEKING OUT THE "DISAPPEARED": ON TRUTH, RECONCILIATION, AND ENGAGING PHILOSOPHY IN HISTORY AS A CULTURAL PRACTICE

History as cultural practice involves looking at what exists in each moment of time that influences how individuals and groups respond in the next. I do not mean this literally as a moment-by-moment study but rather as an orientation of what is involved in change over time. Trying to explain why and how people do the things they do requires an understanding of how they might experience the world. This involves questions that are the province of philosophy, questions regarding cosmology, theories of change, sense of personhood and agency, notions of causality, to name a few. As my colleagues Randall Curren and Charles Dorn argue elsewhere in this volume, a project of this magnitude is necessarily transdisciplinary and collaborative. In this final section, I propose some very modest and provisional proposals based on the vexing questions that have come up in my own work.

If our goal is to create a more expansive context in which to understand historical processes, the first question to ask ourselves is: who are the actors who are missing or silent in our existing historical accounts? There are some historical actors whose presence has been consciously obliterated from the historical record, such as the experiences of LGTBQ persons (Terry 1991). In other cases, one has to know where to look for them. Stephen Haymes (2001, 2008), for instance, has not only found traces of slave and freed blacks perspectives in the biographies they left behind but also makes a compelling argument for why these narratives should be examined as examples of an Africana philosophy, much the way feminist historians such as Mary Spongberg have been tracing women's theorizing through Enlightenment-era biographies (Spongberg 2016).

As we begin to look in conventional and unconventional places for traces of the disappeared, our next steps are to try to make sense—however provisionally and however complicated this sense-making process may be—of what they were thinking and doing at the same time that (other) historical and philosophical actors of their time were writing them out of history and philosophy, given the distinct histories of different "disappeared" at different points in time (cf. Burch and Sutherland 2006; Comaroff and Comaroff 1992; Dirks, Eley, and Ortner 1994; Spivak 1988; Terry 1991). We need to ask, "who are the philosophers and meaning makers and how do we know?" Spongberg and Haymes, for example, both base their arguments on the fact that biographies were part of Enlightenment cultural practices reflecting on the larger social order.

When it comes to engaging and/or recovering the thoughts, perspectives, and actions of "the disappeared," María Lugones (2006) reminds us that it requires a "complex communication" that entails "a recognition of the other that does not attempt to assimilate the other into one's own familiar meanings" (75). Lugones is speaking about communication to facilitate coalitions across oppressed groups on the border, where she recognizes liminality as "both a communicative opening and a communicative impasse" (76) resulting from the different experiences that are not only at odds with each other but also often exist in tension with one another, making "the freeing spaces where we attempt to chisel our own faces . . . not readily accessible to each other" (77). Still, what Lugones (1987) refers to as "world travel" and approaching differences with a sense of love and playfulness constitute "methodologies that enable us to shift to the liminal by reading reality as multiple" (Lugones 2006, 79).

> Recognition of another as luminal . . . is a necessary condition for reading their words and gestures differently. If I think you are in a limen, I will know that, at least some of the time, you do not mean what you say but something else. Sometimes, it is the form of what you say that conveys most of the meaning, a form in sharp contrast with the dominant mainstream. But it is not a question merely of the meaning of words. To understand that you are in a limen is to understand that you are not what you are within a structure. It is to know that you have ways of living in disruption of domination. That is, in my mind, a very good beginning toward understanding your liminal world. What we need then is both to be able to recognize liminality and to go from recognition to a deciphering of resistant codes. (79)

While we may not all stand in a borderland, Lugones raises a question that suggests how we might engage in discourse about a liminal space when one is not actually "from there": can we perceive our own practices as contingent and contextual and go further to imagine how they might look to a world traveler (DeVault and Gross 2011; see Lugones 1987, 2006)?

Lugones's notion of complex communication thus contributes to what Yancy (2015) views as "an expression of larger processes of epistemic decolonization and epistemic liberation" that have "freeing implications for Western philosophy, especially as it takes itself as the hub of universal thought... [offering] the gift of second-sight which is capable of instilling... a productive form of white double consciousness" (1149). Although Yancy (2015) is speaking about what we can learn from seeing the world through the "second sight" of those living with racial marginalization, this awareness arises more generally from collective and individual experiences of living as "deviant" (Lugones 2006; Terry 1991).

How do we begin to think about how historical actors made sense of and gave expression to their experiences when, as in the case of LGBTQ or individuals and groups long deceased, we may not have access to their perspectives unmediated by the discourses that disappeared them or constructed them as deviant in the first place? There may be instances where the "vexing and productive tensions" (Stone-Mediatore 1998) in our work—and who gets to participate in those discussions—may matter more than "getting it right." After all, our preoccupation with solipsism "presuppose[s] a range of implicit assumptions about the self, the world, and one's lived experiences" (Yancy 2015, 1150).

To engage in historical practice as complex communication is akin to the spirit of truth telling employed in the work of truth and reconciliation as in the case of the "disappeared" in Chile and Argentina. The purpose of truth telling is not only to find out what happened to those disappeared by regimes of silence but also to vindicate their very existence. Much like the work of recuperation and re-presentation of African and working-class vernacular art described by Okafor-Newsum (2016) in his study of Neo-Ancestralist artists, commitments to complex communication as truth and reconciliation "serve as metaphors for counterhegemonic strategies of social change" (135).

Archbishop Desmond Tutu reflected that while truth and reconciliation exposes the awfulness of the past it can sometimes make things worse, at least in the short term. We should expect this to be messy. We should expect that we will have to live with the loss of some of our certainties. But in the end, we will gain an expanded sense of the human actors and the values, practices, beliefs, and dispositions that have shaped educational problems, solutions, and processes over time.

REFERENCES

Anzaldúa, Gloria. 1987. *Borderlands: The New Mestiza = La frontera*. San Francisco: Spinsters / Aunt Lute.

Avruch, Kevin. 2006. "Toward and Expanded 'Canon' of Negotiation Theory: Identity, Ideological and Values-Based Conflict and the Need for a New Heuristic." *Marquette Law Review* 89 (3): 567–82.

Balslev, Anindita Niyogi. 1991. *Cultural Otherness: Correspondence with Richard Rorty*. New Delhi: Indian Institute of Advanced Study.
Bernasconi, Robert. 2003. "Hegel's Racism." *Radical Philosophy* 119:35–37.
———. 2016. "China on Parade: Hegel's Manipulation of His Sources and His Change of Mind." In *China in the German Enlightenment*, edited by Bettina Brandt and Daniel Leonhard Purdy, 165–80. Toronto: University of Toronto Press.
Bourdieu, Pierre. 1977. *Outline of a Theory of Practice*. Cambridge: Cambridge University Press.
Brandt, Bettina, and Daniel Leonhard Purdy. 2016. "Introduction." In *China in the German Enlightenment*, edited by Bettina Brandt and Daniel Leonhard Purdy, 1–19. Toronto: University of Toronto Press.
Burch, Susan, and Ian Sutherland. 2006. "Who's Not Yet Here? American Disability History." *Radical History Review* 94:127–47.
Clifford, James. 1988. *The Predicament of Culture: Twentieth-Century Ethnography, Literature and Art*. Cambridge, MA: Harvard University Press.
Comaroff, John, and Jean Comaroff. 1992. *Ethnography and the Historical Imagination*. Boulder, CO: Westview.
Demel, Walter. 2016. "How the Chinese Became Yellow: A Contribution to the Early History of Race Theorie." In *China in the German Enlightenment*, edited by Bettina Brandt and Daniel Leonhard Purdy, 20–59. Toronto: University of Toronto Press.
DeVault, Marjorie L., and Glenda Gross. 2011. "Experience, Talk, and Knowledge." In *Handbook of Feminist Research: Theory and Praxis*. 2nd ed., edited by Sharlene Nagy Hesse-Biber, 206. Los Angeles: SAGE.
Dirks, Nicholas B., George Eley, and Sherry B. Ortner. 1994. *Culture/Power/History: A Reader in Contemporary Social Theory*. Princeton, NJ: Princeton University Press.
Donato, Ruben, and Marvin Lazerson. 2000. "New Directions in American Educational History: Problems and Prospects." *Educational Researcher* 29 (8): 4–15.
Du Bois, William Edward Burghardt. 1897. *Strivings of the Negro People*. Boston: Atlantic Monthly.
Dussel, Enrique. 1996. "Modernity, Eurocentrism, and Trans-modernity: In Dialogue with Charles Taylor." In *The Underside of Modernity: Apel, Ricoeur, Rorty, Taylor, and the Philosophy of Liberation*. Atlantic Highlands, NJ: Humanities.
Eze, Emmanuel Chukwudi. 1997. "The Color of Reason: The Idea of 'Race' in Kant's Anthropology." In *Postcolonial African Philosophy: A Critical Reader*, edited by Emmanuel Chukwudi Eze, 103–31. Cambridge, MA: Blackwell.
———. 2001. "African Philosophy and the Analytic Tradition." *Philosophical Papers* 30 (3): 205–13.
Fleury, Stephen, and Jim Garrison. 2014. "Toward a New Philosophical Anthropology of Education: Fuller Considerations of Social Constructivism." *Interchange (0826–4805)* 45 (1/2):19–41. doi: 10.1007/s10780-014-9216-4.
Goldman, Loren. 2015. "Richard Rorty's 'Post-Kantian' Philosophy of History." *Journal of the Philosophy of History* 9 (3): 410–43. doi: 10.1163/18722636-12341310.
Haymes, Stephen Nathan. 2001. "'Us Ain't Hogs, Us Is Human Flesh': Slave Pedagogy and the Problem of Ontology in African American Slave Culture." *Educational Studies* 32 (2): 129–57.
———. 2008. "Response: Thoughts about the Absence of Africana Philosophy in Philosophy of Education." *Philosophy of Education Yearbook*, 153–56.
Kim, Kyung-Man. 2014. "Beyond Justification: Habermas, Rorty and the Politics of Cultural Change." *Theory, Culture and Society* 31 (6): 103–23.
Kuykendall, Ronald. 1993. "Hegel and Africa." *Journal of Black Studies* 23 (4): 571.
Lugones, María. 1987. "Playfulness, 'World'-Travelling, and Loving Perception." *Hypatia* 2 (2): 3–19.
———. 2006. "On Complex Communication." *Hypatia* 21 (3): 75–85.
Martinez, Jacqueline M. 2014. "Culture, Communication, and Latina Feminist Philosophy: Toward a Critical Phenomenology of Culture." *Hypatia: A Journal of Feminist Philosophy* 29 (1): 221–36.

Mills, Charles W. 1998. "Reply to Critics." *Small Axe: A Caribbean Journal of Criticism* 2 (2): 191.

———. 2002. "The Racial Contract as Methodology (Not Hypothesis)." *Philosophia Africana* 5 (1) : 75.

Okafor-Newsum, H. Ike. 2016. *Soulstirrers: Black Art and the Neo-Ancestral Impulse*. Jackson: University of Mississippi Press.

Outlaw, Lucius T. 1996. *On Race and Philosophy*. London: Routledge.

Oyedola, David A. 2015. "The Culture-Oriented Bias of African Philosophical Inquiry." *Journal of Pan African Studies* 7 (8): 97–109.

Perkins, Franklin. 2016. "Leibniz on the Existence of Philosophy in China." In *China in the German Enlightenment*, edited by Bettina Brandt and Daniel Leonhard Purdy, 60–79. Toronto: University of Toronto Press.

Scott, Joan W. 1993. "'The Evidence of Experience.' The Evidence of Experience." In *The Lesbian and Gay Studies Reader*, edited by Henry Abelove, Michele Aina Barale, and David M. Halperin. New York: Routledge.

Spivak, Gayatri Chakravorty. 1988. "Can the Subaltern Speak?" In *Marxism and the Interpretation of Culture*, edited by Cary Nelson and Lawrence Grossberg. Urbana: University of Illinois Press.

Spongberg, Mary. 2016. "Representing Woman: Historicizing Women in the Age of the Enlightenment." In *Representing Humanity in the Age of Enlightenment*, edited by Alexander Cook, 27–39. New York: Routledge.

Stone-Mediatore, Shari. 1998. "Chandra Mohanty and the Revaluing of 'Experience.'" *Hypatia* 13 (2): 116–33.

Tartaglia, James. 2014. "Rorty's Thesis of the Cultural Specificity of Philosophy." *Philosophy East and West* 64 (4): 1018–38.

Terry, Jennifer. 1991. "Theorizing Deviant Historiography." *differences: A Journal of Feminist Cultural Studies* 3 (2): 55–74.

Yancy, George. 2015. "Through the Crucible of Pain and Suffering: African-American Philosophy as a Gift and the Countering of the Western Philosophical Metanarrative." *Educational Philosophy and Theory* 47 (11): 1143–59.

Chapter Ten

James Bryant Conant, Science, and Science Education

The Uses of History and Philosophy

Wayne J. Urban and Sarah E. Wever

James Bryant Conant, chair of the Harvard University chemistry department, was chosen as president of Harvard University in 1933. He served in that capacity for twenty years, leaving Harvard to become the U.S. high commissioner to West Germany early in 1953. His presidency was marked by a vision of excellence for students and faculty as the sign of a model university. Conant's own summation of his presidency might be found in his final presidential report. In it, he remarks: "Solvency, a student body of high quality, and an outstanding faculty are the three requisites for the successful operation of a university" (Conant 1952, 14).

Trained as a chemist, Conant distinguished himself in the sciences outside of the field of chemistry, particularly in the area of science education, after becoming the president of Harvard. His views on science education were informed by what was then a visionary philosophical and historically grounded understanding of scientific method.

CONANT'S VIEWS ON THE HISTORY OF SCIENCE

From the beginning of his presidency, Conant's entry into most curricular discussions in the 1930s was, unexpectedly for a scientist, through the social sciences. Conant speaks of the importance of a historical understanding of the university, and of the academic scholarship that was its fundamental activity, as a way to mitigate the feuds between academic departments on turf issues by "an appeal to a common family tradition," adding that the "line of descent is the same for all." He notes that, for a genuine development of the history of scholarship, "it is first necessary to train the future professors of this much neglected subject."

Given that academic research and scholarship was most advanced as an enterprise in the natural sciences, to accomplish the objective of charting and understanding that development, he announced that in the academic year 1935–1936 Harvard had established a PhD program in the "history of science and learning." Those responsible for the new doctoral degree were also developing a new field of concentration for a few "undergraduates of high rank" in the history of science. Careful experimentation by teachers of this subject should lead, states Conant, to a demonstration of the "value of the History of Science as a part of the college curriculum for any large body of students" (Conant 1936, 7–8).

Prefiguring his own involvement in history of science courses for nonscientists in the next decade, Conant adds: "I can conceive of a course in the History of Science elected by large numbers of students without scientific bent which ... could serve as an introduction for non-scientists to the methods of science" (Conant 1936, 9). Thus, Conant the chemist, who no longer maintained a program of research in chemistry, found an outlet for his scientific endeavors in advocating and developing the history of science at the graduate and undergraduate levels. In the early 1940s, he helped create a new program in general education for Harvard College students that would enrich the curriculum with rigorous, basic studies in three families of intellectual fields—the humanities, social sciences, and natural sciences.

GENERAL EDUCATION

Conant was frustrated by the intellectual weakness of the distribution requirements that accompanied the system of major and minor concentrations in the Harvard College curriculum. Concentrations were acceptable to Conant, though he was not particularly enthusiastic about them. Nebulous distribution requirements, however, which could be fulfilled through taking any number of courses not developed to serve general education purposes, were in need of replacement.

In his autobiography, Conant recounts the genesis of the Harvard program on general education in the early 1940s: "The idea occurred to us that if the scientists could take time off from their research interests and normal duties to do applied research for the government, why could not a group of professors devote themselves to drawing up plans for education in the postwar world?" (Conant 1970, 364). To accomplish this task, Conant appointed a committee of the Harvard faculty to produce a report on general education.

Conant wrote a substantial introduction to the published report of the Harvard Committee on General Education in which he reveals a good bit of his own thinking about the importance of the topic. He discusses the meaning of the term when he notes: "The heart of the problem of a general education is the continuance of the liberal and humane tradition. Neither the mere acquisition of information nor the development of special skills and talents can give the broad basis of understanding which is essential if our civilization is to be preserved" (Conant 1945, viii). The report, then, was seeking the understanding that would underlie effective, scientifically informed, democratic citizenship in the modern world.

The Harvard committee discussed general education in secondary education, college and university education, and adult education. In a chapter on general education at Harvard College, the committee advocated new general education courses for Harvard undergraduates. Conant himself offered to teach one of the new general education courses in the sciences and proceeded to develop the course of study for that course, titled Natural Science 4. He describes his actions as a way of indicating his clear endorsement of the new general education curriculum. Additionally, he notes that his actions were related to a long-held desire to "demonstrate a way of presenting science to laymen." (Conant 1970, 272).

Conant published two volumes on his development and teaching of Natural Science 4 and also had the actual syllabi of his and other natural science general education courses published (Conant 1947, 1949, 1950, 1957). These volumes testify to Conant's unwillingness to discard his professional adherence to the sciences while explaining the reasons for such an adherence to nonscientists. His courses were grounded in the history of science, a testimony to his long-standing interest in historical studies for the larger intellectual and social benefit they offered.

The prime objectives of Conant's general education science course was to show students science's relationship with other fields as well as to provide a grounding from which to understand current problems and issues requiring scientific knowledge. Teaching science to nonscientists was a difficult but not impossible task. Conant's appeal to the human drama often involved in scientific discovery helped him reach students. He wanted scientific understanding to be a part of a student's larger intellectual stance, one that related scientific developments to intellectual and cultural history (Conant 1949, 2–4).

Conant describes his general education course in science as a study of the tactics and strategy of science, an area for which he believed intelligent nonscientists had "no feel" (Conant 1947, 12). This lack of feel for the topic was made worse by some in the natural and social sciences who argued that, "modern science as training the mind to be an exact and impartial analysis of facts is an education specially fitted to promote sound citizenship." For Conant, this analysis "put the scientist on a pedestal because he is an impartial inquirer."

In fact, in the early stages of the development of many sciences, according to Conant, "prejudice and vanity proved stumbling blocks to progress." Early scientists often stumbled on their way to a discovery, hampered by poor formulations, prejudices, and misleading generalization. While more recently the professionalization of science had alleviated this situation a bit, there was no reason to put any absolute trust in the scientific method or in scientists.

He adds: "My observations lead me to conclude that as human beings scientific investigators are statistically distributed over the whole spectrum of human folly and wisdom much as other men." He concludes that to "claim that the study of science is the best education for young men who aspire to become impartial analysts of human affairs is to put forward a very dubious educational hypothesis at best" (Conant 1947, 6, 10, 15).

Conant's specific target here was the view that scientific rigor was the key to understanding and solving social problems and issues. This notion of science as the ultimate way to human improvement was deeply flawed, according to Conant. The flaw came from seeing and studying science logically or philosophically, seeking generalizations that would hold in all situations. Conant's approach to science was not philosophical but historical or empirical. He thought that such a study of science led both to an appreciation of its accomplishments and their contextualization in ways that would expose the foibles of science and scientists as well as the accidents and other unplanned factors related to scientific discovery.

Conant advocated study of particular cases in the history of science, chosen specifically to illustrate the uneven development of science, the human factors that influenced science, and the role of chance and other unexplained or unexplainable factors in the process. He relied on early cases in the history of science for study in his course, rather than more recent ones, because of their ease of accessibility to nonscientists. The cases that he chose did not require technical knowledge or mathematical skills to be understood by the student.

Conant's cases emphasize two other factors not usually prominent in science teaching. The first was the inclusion of the practical knowledge and concerns involved in scientific discoveries, an emphasis downplayed in science courses that focused mainly on the growth of science itself. The mundane and the practical, for Conant and his cases, were every bit as important as the theoretical in explaining scientific discovery. Secondly, he remarks that he paid attention to "the less spectacular and the less known advances in the sciences," since more "can be learned from their study than from the few famous sweeping generalizations which in their time gathered up so much of the past and illumined the future so brightly" (Conant 1947, 21).

The initial publication of the specific cases involved in Conant's course describe three cases: Robert Boyle's experiments in pneumatics, the "overthrow of the phlogiston theory," and the early developments in the concepts of "temperature and heat." In each case, as one reviewer notes, emphasis is placed on "the methodological aspects of the research and the influence of social factors on the development of physical science." The reviewer concludes that the approach to these cases holds "great promise," especially if new cases are added that involve the biological as well as the physical sciences and the social sciences as well. Such additions would "help dispel the misconception that scientific rigor is an exclusive possession of the physical sciences, and that scientific progress is an exclusive contribution of these same sciences" (R. L. A. 1953).

Conant was more reticent than the reviewer to expand on the value of his cases to other fields. Conant was, however, interested in discussing how knowledge about the sciences that students took away from his course would be helpful in a larger effort in the social sciences. Specifically, despite his earlier contentions about the sometimes serendipitous nature of scientific discovery, he notes: "We need to lay the basis for a better discussion of the ways in which rational methods may be applied to the study and solution of human problems" (Conant 1947, 5).

In an exchange with a Harvard sociologist about the applicability of natural science to social science, he remained a skeptic. While he thought that there certainly had been advances in statistics, demography, and psychological testing, the advances were "empirical, not theoretical." Furthermore, the sociologist's recommendation to concentrate Harvard's work in pure social science research was one with which he strongly disagreed. According to Conant, echoing a point made about the natural sciences in his course, "Only from practical problems can material come that will advance your science" (Keller and Keller 2001, 93).

EXTENDING THE REACH OF GENERAL EDUCATION IN SCIENCE

Conant taught his course for three years in the late 1940s. It reinforced his reputation as a noted American scientist, though no longer a research chemist. He enhanced his reputation as a scientist with the publication of a volume on science in the early 1950s, where he extended his Harvard general education in science work by addressing a larger lay public on the nature of science. *Science and Common Sense* (1951) was originally intended to be a second edition of a small book detailing Conant's work on his general education course, *On Understanding Science*, published in 1947.

However, he describes *Science and Common Sense* as "a much larger book on the methods of science for the general reader." In the first chapter, he notes that "this is a citizen's guide to the methods of experimental science . . . addressed to the intelligent citizen who, as a voter may, to an increasing extent, be interested in congressional action on scientific matters" (Conant 1951, vi, 1).

Conant here again criticizes those who believe that rigorous, experimental scientists utilizing a codified scientific method are paragons of rationality in the modern world. For Conant, there is no single scientific method based on measurement or experiments that results in scientific progress and accomplishments. Rather, close attention to past progress in science shows that advance is halting, based on observation, intuition, and criticism and on speculative reasoning and deduction.

All of this was related to practical concerns advanced by nonscientists such as artisans and agriculturists, who were focused on the solution of practical problems. He also felt that the significance of scientific societies in earlier centuries and universities in his own time needed to be acknowledged. Conant's point, as foreshadowed in the title of this work, is that science and common sense are intimately related to each other. Conant refuses to grant the experimental scientist a privileged status in public discourse.

In addition to the cases he had used in his Harvard course, he adds cases from biology and geology in this volume. For the layman, the lesson of the cases is that the "great working hypotheses in the past have often originated in the minds of the pioneers as a result of mental processes which can best be described by such words as 'inspired guess,' 'intuitive hunch,' or 'brilliant flash of imagination'" (Conant 1951, 48).

While Conant did not want to call into doubt the technical attributes of scientists, he did want readers to understand that, regardless of their expertise, scientists were not the sole, or even the most important, arbiters of scientific progress. He phrases his point this way: "In following my exposition of the methods of experimental science by using examples from the past, the reader must be asked to become as much of a skeptic about scientific explanations as he can." He adds: "Experimental science can be thought of as an activity which increases the adequacy of the concept and conceptual schemes which are related to certain types of perception and which lead to certain types of activities; *it is one extension of common sense*" (Conant 1951, 31–32).

Rather than be intimidated by science, Conant wanted lay people to appreciate scientific advancements while understanding the many extra-scientific attributes that led to them. It was easy to show science as an extension of common sense historically, since the early discoveries were not shrouded in technical complexities. But, for Conant, even in the increasingly complex science of the twentieth century, the relationship of science to common sense should not be ignored. He opines that "we start with the historic connection between common sense and science and follow these implications to the aspects of modern science (which are manifold) where the relation has hardly changed in this century." The contingency of scientific accomplishment was important to Conant, as was its relationship to practical and organizational concerns and its dependence on chance occurrences and the careful observation of those occurrences (Conant 1951, 27).

Conant insists on contingency, intuition, deduction, and other extra-experimental concerns and qualities because he wanted the layman to become involved in discussions of science and its practical uses, exceedingly important concerns in the middle of the twentieth century. Conant's view of science was that of a dynamic enterprise rather than as some static and progressive accumulation of knowledge. "Science is an interconnected series of concepts and conceptual schemes that have developed as a result of experimentation and observation and are fruitful of further experimentation and observations. In this definition the emphasis is on the word 'fruitful.' Science is a speculative enterprise" (Conant 1951, 25).

Conant intended that his main points about the natural sciences also be applied to the social sciences and their impact on social affairs. Conant believed in the potential of the social sciences and was interested in what they might contribute to social welfare. He was not, however, one who would look to the social sciences for direction in social affairs. He thought that they could "benefit social organization and welfare, but not as easily as natural sciences impact economy and warfare."

He adds that one "should have no illusion that basic national issues can be handled by any group of social scientists in the way that problems of design of bridges and machines can be treated by engineers. Policy questions must be resolved, in the future as in the past, by governmental officials, business executives, and labor leaders; they cannot be handed over to scientific experts to find an answer which is 'right'" (Conant 1951, 343). Policy decisions also needed to be informed by the insights of historians who added to the consideration of present policy the conduct and outcome of past policies and by social philosophers who helped historians and social scientists to interpret the meaning of their work.

Yet, Conant was not dismissive of the social sciences. He adds that they could be helpful in social policy, particularly in consideration of the "types of problems where one can hope for help from the social psychologist, sociologist, and anthropologist," namely those involving "human relations and those conflicts among individuals and groups which have been so much intensified by the conditions of modern life" (Conant 1951, 344).

Above all, Conant wanted natural science and social science to be subject to scrutiny by the larger American public. The political context for Conant's concern was the burgeoning Cold War, made much warmer through the conflict in Korea, which was between competing social systems of communism and democracy. In this conflict, he felt scientific progress would be impeded "if the general public fails to understand the significance of free publication and discussion" (Conant 1951, 348). For Conant, it was that discussion and wide dissemination of science and social science that distinguished democracy from communism.

In spite of Conant's intention to have his ideas on science applied to the social sciences and disseminated to a general lay audience, the reviews of *Science and Common Sense* came largely from within the scientific community. Two of the most extensive reviews, both largely favorable, came from a history of science journal and a biology journal. The first, by a noted botanist who also worked in the history of science, sees Conant's work as an endorsement of a true liberal education as the way for a layperson to begin to understand and participate in public affairs. Its major criticism is that the case method, used appropriately by Conant, is not the only, or even the most useful, way to get a good grip on science and its contributions (Zirkle 1951, 268–71).

The biological science journal review, written by an affiliate of the Zoological Laboratory at Yale, endorses Conant's declaration that there is no such thing as a single scientific method as well as his nuanced discussion and critique of the role of quantification and measurement in science. The reviewer also approves of Conant's desire to distinguish scientific concepts from experiments and other aspects of empirical/experimental science but adds that scientists themselves are not always aware of this distinction. This review also applauds Conant's rigorous views of the limitations of the contributions that science and scientists make to human affairs. Finally, the end of the review reiterates Conant's stress on the importance of understanding science to informed citizens in a free society (Oppenheimer 1951, 364–66).

Two other reviews of *Science and Common Sense*, one in a higher-education journal and the other in a sociology journal, give some evidence that Conant might be reaching an academic audience outside of the sciences, though not the lay audience he desired. The brief review of Conant's book in the *Journal of Higher Education* is headed with the words "Helpful Reorientation." The reviewer goes on to stress Conant's view of science as a speculative enterprise and concludes by noting that the last two chapters deal effectively with issues related to science and government and private industry. These matters were of special interest to university administrators, causing the reviewer to conclude with the following evaluation: "This book should have value for the general reader, but its major contribution will be in helping university educators to reorient scientific education into more fertile and effective modes of operation" (Tead 1951, 453–54).

The reviewer in the sociological journal applauds Conant's inclusion of the social sciences, especially sociology, in his analysis. He applauds Conant's major thesis about science and notes that the tendency of science to be on occasion too empirical and on other occasions too theoretical is shared by the discipline of sociology. Conant's inclusion of social science in his analysis is, the reviewer hopes, a sign that the social sciences might be able to overcome their exclusion by the National Science Foundation from research support.

The reviewer adds that Conant has changed his mind on the social sciences "during the last four or five years." (Barber 1951, 736). Yet Conant, from the first decade of his presidency, was interested in both the history of science and history and the social sciences. In the second decade of that presidency, he promoted innovations in the social sciences such as the creation of the general education program in an attempt to make Harvard a leader in social science research and teaching. The important point here is that Conant was widening the academic audience for his work in raising conceptual and practical concerns about science and social science, though he was not necessarily reaching the lay audiences he expressly addressed in his volume.

CONCLUSION

We have consciously proceeded in this chapter inductively, as Conant did in his science education course, beginning with Conant's actions at Harvard in the 1930s promoting history and the history of science, proceeding to his involvement in the general education program and the development of his general education course in science, and ending with his publication for a lay audience of *Science and Common Sense*. In this conclusion, we contextualize Conant's work in terms of other work like it done at Harvard during his time there.

In a recent discussion of what he calls the "human sciences" at Harvard University between the 1920s and the 1960s, Joel Isaac (2012) argues that the major progress in those areas came not through work in the academic departments and disciplines but, rather, through work in what he calls an "intramural gray zone of marginal professional schools, special seminars, interfaculty discussion groups, and non-professionalized societies and teaching programs."

He describes these "interstitial, under institutionalized academic spaces" as places where the "identification of epistemology with pedagogy and research practice offered a means of defending the integrity of the human sciences." In this "set of irregular institutional arrangements and the attitudes toward science and knowledge that those institutions fostered, . . . epistemology was embodied by and sustained in practices of pedagogy and inquiry" (6).

Isaac's book is part of a wave of work in the "human sciences," basically a larger category than social sciences that allows for transfer of knowledge and understanding between some of the natural sciences and the social sciences not unlike a good bit of what Conant discusses in his own work (Ross 2014, 191–209). It is not the place here to discuss either Isaac's Harvard or the human sciences at length.

It is, however, enough to mention that work as providing an intellectual context within which Conant operated, a context not particularly valued in an academic setting dominated by disciplines and departments. Conant was not anti-discipline or anti-department; however, he thought that their place was mainly in graduate education and not in undergraduate education or in professional schools.

He worked hard to insulate the general education programs that he valued from dominance by departments and disciplines that would work against their objective of liberalizing knowledge and the undergraduate student consumers of that knowledge. Conant is a recurring figure in Isaac's account of Harvard, particularly in his activities in sponsoring the general education program, teaching a course in it, and writing about it for larger audiences than Harvard. In all of this work, Conant was active as a developer of Isaac's "working knowledge," the constellation of pedagogical and research activities that took place outside of the normal departmental and disciplinary channels at Harvard and that formed much of the creative accomplishment in the human sciences that took place there.

And, to further illustrate Conant's association with the creative intellectual processes at Harvard, consider perhaps the signature volume in the human sciences in the mid-twentieth century. Arguably, this volume was *The Structure of Scientific Revolutions*, by Thomas S. Kuhn. Kuhn got his start in the history and philosophy of science at Harvard as a teaching assistant to James Bryant Conant in Natural Science 4, Conant's general education course. Their relationship was more than that of a graduate student and his teacher. At least, that is what we conclude from the fact that *The Structure of Scientific Revolutions* is dedicated to James Bryant Conant (Kuhn 1962).

REFERENCES

Barber, Bernard. 1951. "Review of *Science and Common Sense* by James B. Conant." *American Sociological Review* 16 (October): 735–36.

Conant, James B. 1935–1936. Presidential Reports, 7–9. Harvard University Library.

———. 1945. Report of the Harvard Committee. "Introduction by James Bryant Conant." In *General Education in a Free Society*, viii. Cambridge, MA: Harvard University Press.

———. 1947. "Dwight Harrington Tarry Foundation, Lectures on Religion in the Light of Science and Philosophy." In *On Understanding Science*. New Haven, CT: Yale University Press.

———. 1949. *The Growth of the Experimental Sciences: An Experiment in General Education: Progress Report on the Use of the Case Method in Teaching the Principles of the Tactics and Strategy of Science*. Cambridge, MA: Harvard University Press.

———. 1950. *Harvard Case Histories in Experimental Science*. Cambridge, MA: Harvard University Press.

———. 1951. *Science and Common Sense*. New Haven, CT: Yale University Press.

———. 1951–1952. Presidential Reports, 14. Harvard University Library.

———. 1970. *My Several Lives: Memoirs of a Social Inventor*. New York: Harper and Row.

Conant, James Bryant, ed. et al. 1957. *Harvard Case Histories in Experimental Science*. Cambridge, MA: Harvard University Press.

Isaac, Joel. 2012. *Working Knowledge: Making the Human Sciences from Parsons to Kuhn*. Cambridge, MA: Harvard University Press.

Keller, Morton, and Phyllis Keller. 2001. *Making Harvard Modern: The Rise of the Modern University*. New York: Oxford University Press.

Kuhn, Thomas S. 1962. *The Structure of Scientific Revolutions*. Chicago: University of Chicago Press.

Oppenheimer, Jane. 1951. "Review of *Science and Common Sense* by James B. Conant." *Quarterly Review of Biology* 26 (December): 364–66.

R. L. A. 1953. "Review of *Harvard Case Histories in Experimental Science*," *Philosophy of Science* 20 (October): 346.

Ross, Dorothy. 2014. "Getting over It: From the Social Sciences to the Human Sciences." *Modern Intellectual History* 11 (April): 191–209.

Tead, Ordway. 1951. "Review of *Science and Common Sense* by James B. Conant." *Journal of Higher Education* 22 (November): 453–54.

Zirkle, Conway. 1951. "Review of *Science and Common Sense* by James B. Conant." *Isis* 42 (October): 268–71.

Chapter Eleven

History and Philosophy of Education as "Pre Qualitative" Educational Research

Samuel D. Rocha

"The age of hospital medicine, which from rise to fall lasted no more than a century and a half, is coming to an end."
—Ivan Illich, *Limits to Medicine*

Historians and philosophers of education are presently outnumbered in the field of education by a wide and widening margin. From the shrinking size of professional societies to the meager allocation of grants and rare availability of jobs and, of course, the few specializing graduate programs still in existence to the scant course offerings in educational research and teacher education programs and more: all relevant and well-known indicators suggest that the scale of history and philosophy of education—even when combined—is miniscule by comparison to the social scientific disciplines within the educational field at large.[1]

The analogy exists sufficiently to suggest that being a historian or philosopher of education in the academic field of education today is to be like an institutional minority of some kind.

I feel the marginal state of my discipline in the field of education in various ways. The most depressing way, far worse than the mere risk of total extinction, appears when I have to argue for the idea that there is research in education that is not social scientific in nature. I cannot count the times that I have seen a colleague or a student look at me with shock, surprise, and even wonder at the prospect that there is educational research that does not fit into the quantitative, qualitative, and mixed methodological trinity. Many times students ask me if this is really true, in that incredulous way one might question a miracle or a magic trick. "You mean I don't have to do interviews?"

In more sympathetic cases, I am told that my story is similar to many accounts of multidisciplinary qualitative researchers. I must admit that I often envy the lowly yet at least imaginable state of even the most obscure qualitative research. However powerless and rare qualitative researchers may be in relation to psychometricians these days in education, they are at the very least established enough to be dismissed in a voluntary act of *commission* by their quantitative peers. For the historian or philosopher of education, the dismissal is usually, by contrast, one of involuntary *omission*.

This introduces the preoccupation that motivates this chapter and I think it is easily tested in a negative way. There are no historians or philosophers of education of present or recent memory that see themselves as being numerous in relation to the now vast field of social scientific educational researchers. Likewise, there is no one in the field of education who would suggest that the disciplines of history and philosophy of education are growing too large or even growing at all. To make matters more complex, many historians and philosophers of education are forced to pretend to be qualitative researchers to work and survive, often teaching methods that are not proper to their discipline or training. I am sure many of them doing empirical research choose to do so freely, but I am also certain that the strategic advantages of that approach are not lost on them.

In the sections to follow, I would like to try to accomplish two things in response to the situation I have outlined thus far. First, I hope to sketch a preliminary sense of the historical context for the present state of the disciplines of history and philosophy of education within the academic field of education. This will include some critical attention to the particular case made by John Dewey for the legitimation of education as a university discipline in the late nineteenth century—a case often overlooked by philosophers of education who assume that Dewey's educational interests were primarily philosophical and humanistic. Secondly, I hope to point toward a contemporary movement in qualitative educational research and curriculum theory exemplified by Elizabeth Adams St. Pierre's interesting appeal for what she calls "post qualitative research" (2011). Here, in this recent departure of social science from itself, I will suggest that history and philosophy of education may find some sure footing, correcting foundational missteps of Dewey's scientific agenda for education. In between points one and two, I will interject a dose of balance from William James to avoid the mistake of overdetermination in my two speculative main points. In sum, I am suggesting what amounts to an alternative as old as it is new to historians and philosophers of education and anyone weary with the inability of social scientific inquiry to keep its promises.

DEWEY

At first glance, the introductory tone of this chapter may seem to invite persecution or conspiracy theories. I hope to dispel this impression by looking directly to the historical beginnings of the field of education as an academic subject and discipline in the university, propelled in large measure by the well-known patron saint of philosophy of education, John Dewey. After a look at what seem to be ignored details about the nature of Dewey's advocacy for education as a field unto itself in the late nineteenth century, I will in the next section contrast this from the approach of his contemporary during that period, William James.

Dewey's early work from the 1880s to the 1900s was consistently aimed at making the study of education a field of its own with proper academic respectability. The two most representative arguments from both ends of the spectrum come from his September 1896 article in the *University of Chicago Record* titled "Pedagogy as a University Discipline" and his 1907 article in the *Columbia University Quarterly* titled "Education as a University Study." One can find a progression across each article's argument, from a specific advocacy of a more professionalized pedagogy to an appeal to consider education as a self-sufficient field more broadly speaking. This second emphasis creates some confusion to this day among historians and philosophers of education alike, since the historical or philosophical study of education can be done in either the "home disciplines" or in a department or school of education. There is no consensus on where it is that a historian or philosopher of education belongs, in principle or in practice, but one thing worth noting is that Dewey, in this time, was not exclusively or even principally a philosopher and much less a philosopher of education when it came to his interest in education.

One thing to recall from this period of Dewey, which remained a major influence throughout, is that Dewey was a psychologist. He served as president of the American Psychological Association in 1899 and published three books on the matter in the 1880s until the psychological works of William James surpassed him. With respect to education and pedagogy, Dewey's interests were largely psychological in nature and experimentally so. After all, Dewey's enthusiasm for science was neither a post-Darwinian affectation nor a secondhand endorsement. Dewey himself was a practicing social scientist in the infant field of social psychology, surely motivating his initiative to establish a "laboratory" school—a distinctly scientific designation, appealing to the metaphor of the natural sciences—for the purposes of "child study." Dewey's scientific gusto is well known, yet his work in education is seen as manifestly philosophical in scope, a slight mischaracterization of his social scientific works and of his efforts to legitimize education as a field on scientific grounds. Even in his later work, Dewey returned often to questions that were far more applicable in the domain of social science than in more theoretical questions of the philosophy of science. A notable example of this is his 1931 column in the *New Republic*, "Social Science and Social Control."

What this implies in a very preliminary way is that the earliest educational research in the university, founded by the founder of the field of philosophy of education, was not particularly philosophical or humanistic in scope or approach at that time. This is certainly not to claim that Dewey ever endorsed or practiced an overdetermined reliance on experimental science. Indeed, he argued against this explicitly. But it does reveal that, for Dewey, the study of the school and forms of education was to follow a primarily psychological, scientific regimen. To be clear, there is no comparison in degree between psychology in Dewey's day and the present vulgarities of applied psychometrics today, but there is also little consolation of a purely historical or philosophical conception of the study of education in the ideal past.

Indeed, Dewey's agenda for education as a separate field was not one that existed apart from the humanities; it was not primarily academic in nature. As the professionalism and credentialism of the normal school for teacher training was elevated into the university at large, Dewey conflated professional training and the more academic disciplines as late as the 1931 *New Republic* column mentioned above, which extends into his analogous advocacy for the exceptionality of art in *Art as Experience*. This was a principled and philosophical conflation, and here we observe aspects of Dewey's pragmatism, which would deny the distinction between applied and theorized knowledge as a false binary. However ironic and complex this matrix of social science and philosophy is—a large measure of which is simply a reflection of the historical reality of that time—suffice it to say now that there is no romantic return to a pure humanistic study of education to be found in the institutional history of the university's adoption of education as a field of study unto itself. In other words, Dewey's scientific entanglement with philosophy, which was in many ways an analogy from the biological to the sociological to the pragmatic, prevents my analysis from pretending that a humanistic field of educational research was ever the case historically or conceptually speaking.

This profile contrasts with the enormous influence of Dewey's philosophical works on education, such as *Democracy and Education* (1916). Yet perhaps it ought to contextualize those claims rather than subvert them. What seems clear when considering Dewey as a psychologist is that he had significant training in philosophy *before* he took up a scientific research method in his lab school. This is indicative of the attitude of Dewey and, by extension, the early days of the field of education. Primarily for us it reveals a misguided assumption in Dewey's scientific approach: at least in his writing on the matter, he does not seem to recognize—at least not in an educational or curricular way—his own formal study of philosophy as a preparatory antecedent to his interests and research in psychology. Today we also seem to miss this fact. Dewey may advocate for the study of education as an academic discipline, but he seems to miss or simply assume a foundational set of studies that would precede it.

Nonetheless, ipso facto, Dewey's own humanistic and philosophical academic training surely prepared him to conceptualize, defend, and found his lab school and, eventually, the academic field of education. This does not explain or excuse the sense in which the present state of social scientific research in education is in a much different condition, where philosophers are no longer doing the bulk of social scientific research (or where those who do so do it in historically different strategic ways). Yet, Dewey's psychological and social scientific frame of mind at the foundation of the field of education should dispel any inclination to think that the present condition of history and philosophy of education is different from its genealogical origin.

JAMES

Dewey's disciplinary approach to education and unskeptical faith in Modern post-Darwinian science was not the only attitude of its time. While it was surely the most lasting, popular, and influential, and therefore of greatest interest to us now, we find a very different outlook and attitude in the almost cynical sentiment toward "the new psychology" delivered by William James in his 1892 lectures and subsequent book, *Talks to Teachers on Psychology* ([1899] 1962). Consider, for instance, this quotation from James's comments on the state of the booming young fields of psychology and education in relation to teachers:

> "The new psychology" has thus become a term to conjure up portentous ideas withal; and you teachers, docile and receptive and aspiring as many of you are, have been plunged in an atmosphere of vague talk about our science, which to a great extent has been more mystifying than enlightening. Altogether it does seem as if there were a great certain fatality of mystification laid upon the teachers of the day. (James [1899] 1962, 2)

This passage alone conveys a stark difference between two nineteenth-century psychologists and their corresponding attitudes about the role of social science in education and pedagogy. James continues, however, insisting in more succinct terms, "To know psychology, therefore, is absolutely no guarantee that we shall be good teachers" (James [1899] 1962, 3). For James, the presence of social scientific studies for education, psychological, or otherwise was something about which he was agnostic, if not downright contemptuous.

One might be critical of this comparison between Dewey and James because Dewey the psychologist never insisted that teachers should know psychology. For Dewey, it was principally psychology that would gain from observing forms of education. My point in making this comparison, however, is about the respective *attitudes* of Dewey and James toward education and the social sciences. Dewey shows a clear optimism for what the social scientific study of education can do in his lab school, which, I claim, best explains his rationale for arguing that it merits its own field of university study. James, on the other hand, is more suspicious about the new psychology's ability to add value to teaching and, one must assume, the study of education. This explains in some measure why Dewey pursued institutional credibility for the field of education, while James—who himself founded the academic Department of Psychology at Harvard—was content to stay out of the way of teachers, even as he lectured them on his psychological subject matter.

This contrast is suggestive in some ways but does not offer any sense of the present-day situation in constructive terms. To this slightly different task I turn in the section to follow. However, before leaving James behind, it is important to note that James was not trained in the disciplines of philosophy or psychology. His degree was in medicine. This highlights a separate cautionary tale: philosophy of education (I should not speak on behalf of history of education in this case) cannot so easily assume what, exactly, the discipline of *philosophy* is, since it is famously filled with those whose training or specialization is in other areas—or who, like Socrates, do not understand nor practice philosophy as a professional or academic entity at all.

ST. PIERRE

In the fourth edition of the *SAGE Handbook of Qualitative Inquiry*, published in 2011, Elizabeth Adams St. Pierre begins with a note about the degree to which her "post qualitative" position has been in the making for over twenty years. Within the first lines of the opening paragraph, she registers her fatigue: "I am weary . . . of defending an over-determined qualitative inquiry I find increasingly limited" (611). The early impression given by St. Pierre in this chapter is one of a palpable sense of overburden by present forms of qualitative social science research. This fatigue, in her view, demands a "post qualitative" approach to educational research. After documenting the rejection of qualitative research by the demand for "scientifically based research" (SBR) by the National Research Council (NRC) and others who St. Pierre refers to as "positivist and conservative," and then moving to further document the quixotic "resurgence of postmodernism" in light of the SBR movement in educational policy and research, St. Pierre turns against what she calls "conventional humanist qualitative research" (611). She puts her criticism in the following way: "We now have thousands of textbooks, handbooks, and journal articles that have secured *qualitative methodology* by repeating that structure in book after book with the same chapter headings so that we now believe it is real and true. *We've forgotten we made it up*" (613).

The sentiment of her weariness with the formulaic status quo of qualitative research and its organizational buzzwords (e.g., "research question," "methodology," "theoretical framework," and more) resonates strongly with my own worries—despite the fact that I am not nearly as opposed to a host of conventional philosophical traditions or positions—especially when considering her almost confessional remembrance that it is all made up, canonized in the very handbooks in which her new "post qualitative" proposal ironically appears.

This leads St. Pierre to a defense of "theory" that is hard to distinguish from a more specific defense of postmodernism (which she later links with post-structuralism), and here we find the claim I wish to endorse. She writes, "I am convinced that philosophy should precede the study of research methodology" (St. Pierre 2011, 613–14). A bit later she augments that claim, saying, "If we don't read the theoretical and philosophical literature, we have nothing much to think with during analysis except normalized discourses that seldom explain the way things are" (614). In other words, "philosophy," "postmodernism," and "theory" are, for St. Pierre, the social scientific tools for having interesting thoughts that are not normalized by status quo discourse.

St. Pierre's final section of the chapter is subtitled "A Return to Philosophy," which sounds nice enough to my ears but also presupposes that a *return* is possible, an assumption I find difficult to understand. After all, I can return to Ohio State to give a talk because I spent three years there in the past, but I cannot return to China because I have never been to China. As we have seen with Dewey, education as an academic field and university discipline has never been to China. So perhaps what St. Pierre means by a "return to philosophy" is to acknowledge a fundamental "pre qualitative" role of philosophy to social scientists bored and fed up with social science itself. She seems to say as much when she writes in a similarly weary tone as quoted before, "many of us are weary of all the lines drawn around social science inquiry these days" (St. Pierre 2011, 622–23).

St. Pierre ends with "a call for philosophically informed inquiry by inquirers who have read and studied philosophy." This tautological formulation is not a flattering philosophical sentence, nor is it quite as interesting as the fascinatingly abrupt note she leaves the reader with in her final two sentences where she suggestively writes, "It seems we have to keep on learning that philosophy and science are not individuated but always already entangled. The most important task of post qualitative inquiry is to attend to that false and grievous distinction" (623).

In a clarifying interview on her "post qualitative" research program published in 2015, we find a restatement of the basic tenets of her 2011 chapter, especially with respect to the evocative but somewhat abrupt finale cited above. On the place and role of philosophy in her formulation of post qualitative research, St. Pierre offers a notable suggestion, showing that her sense of philosophical and scientific entanglement does not include the *social* sciences at all. She clarifies as follows:

> I think much of this new work is trying to connect educational research and practice back to philosophy and the *natural* sciences, where it has always existed, and to de-center its relation to the social sciences, which, I think, has overwhelmed us and normalized what we think and do. I love working with students who have degrees in philosophy—they have conceptual frameworks to think with. They don't have to rely on the methodologies we teach them to get going. (Guttorm, Hohti, and Paakkari 2015, 17)

The question that remains in this observation is one of degree: to what *degree* does post qualitative research seek to reconnect or return to philosophy and natural science, and why would we not expect the next turn to be a divorce from the scientific educational project championed by Dewey and implied by St. Pierre's post qualitative turn? In her latest article on the matter, titled "Deleuze and Guattari's Language for New Empirical Inquiry," she seems to answer or at least clarify this question. She writes, "The present is the old methodologies of the old empiricisms that we must set aside. But then what? If we call ourselves researchers we might need a method. Perhaps in new empirical work, we might think *concept as method*." (St. Pierre 2016, 8).

This idea of "*concept as method*" echoes certain developments in art, where those like Marina Abramović—and in education those like Jorge Lucero or Rita Irwin—work not so much with matter but with ideas. It goes without saying at this point that the not-so-new-anymore movements of object-oriented ontology, new materialism, and post-humanism have had a field day recently in this arena, and St. Pierre credits her own post-structural readings for her "post qualitative" turn.

However, it would be too quick to make this all quite so fashionable. Philosophy and humanities of all sorts have been doing concept-first work for millennia with few, if any, interruptions. But these types of research, as St. Pierre's advocacy suggests, largely do not exist in the institutional study of education. Whether one is a post-humanist Deleuzian theorist of (im)materiality or a classical Thomistic Dominican monk rereading commentaries on the Trinity—or both!—the humanistic scope and method of this style of research is equally as implausible in education. Perhaps then St. Pierre's "concept as method" could opt to take up social scientific inquiry but could also afford to be agnostic about it—or, like me, a fierce atheist. All the more reason to take St. Pierre's call seriously, if not too seriously, and realize that the very fact that putting concepts before methods can even be called "new" today is a clarion call for the field of education to wake up from the dogmatism of its social scientific slumber—a slumber which of course relies on a uniquely *Modern* conception of science itself.

When we look at St. Pierre herself, we find that she shares a philosophical training with Dewey—her undergraduate degree was in philosophy, something they do not share with James the autodidact. When we look to contemporary eminent scholars in the wider educational field, we often find a humanistic foundation. Bill Pinar's background is in religious studies and literature; Patti Lather's is English; Deborah Britzman, Madeline Grumet, Nel Noddings, and recently passed Maxine Greene's humanistic bona fides go without saying. Critical theory from Frankfurt and Birmingham schools, and also Paulo Freire, are all well detached from the present cookbook style of five-chapter social science.

This all lends significant weight to St. Pierre's claims about the antecedent role of philosophy to qualitative research, and historians and philosophers could extend those claims, asserting themselves as forms of "pre qualitative" research for social science writ large. Historians would provide the most concrete side of the argument, and philosophers would hopefully not entirely spoil it. Surely this would have immediate traction in fields like curriculum theory, where St. Pierre's work is widely cited and known, and also places like art education, where the presence of social science looms heavy, ironic, and absurd.

END OF AN AGE?

For history and philosophy of education to survive in the field of education, the social sciences do not need to die. But we also need not assume that social scientists are thriving to the degree their numbers suggest; the pulse of their vitality may itself be overestimated in education. Whatever the case may be, there is solace and even a spark of enthusiasm at the idea that the field of education has never attempted reorganization around the humanities and, much less, the arts. Perhaps today we have the option to enter the end of the Deweyian Age of education, the age born of progressive faith in the power of science to organize and understand the human condition's relation to education. In this new age, I can only dream that history and philosophy of education take their place preceding qualitative speculation, judgment, and measurement—and that the arts take their corresponding place prior to the metaphysics of humanistic inquiry.

This new age is Deweyian in a some ways, but more importantly, it glimmers with a richer and more capacious ability to take concepts and ideas seriously, which might render concepts of education that imagine education with and without the school, for and from a spirit both immanent and transcendent, ancient and new. Most of all, in this new age of education, education may prove more than something to be invented or studied from afar, something that is not only a concept but also a *reality*. Education itself may have something to teach us that may prove educative to those of us in repeating search (*re*-search) of its meaning and being.

My prayer then is for an epochal conversion, a turning into a new age of educational research, an age much like all ages, an age where the search for education is less limited by the search itself, an age that allows us to dwell in closer and more constant communion with the timely and timeless relationships we form and are formed by when we are educated anew. In an age where the "new" has become quite old, perhaps we ought to allow the "post" to be ordered, again, by the "pre."

REFERENCES

Dewey, John. 1916. *Democracy and Education: An Introduction to the Philosophy of Education*. New York: Macmillan.
Guttorm, H., Hohti, K., and Paakkari A. 2015. "'Do the Next Thing': An Interview with Elizabeth Adams St. Pierre on Post-qualitative Methodology." *Reconceptualizing Educational Research Methodology* 6 (1): 15–22. https://journals.hioa.no/index.php/rerm/article/view/1421/1269.
James, W. (1899) 1962. *Talks to Teachers on Psychology: And to Students on Some of Life's Ideals*. New York: Dover.
Rocha, S. D. 2013. "Unscientific Science and the Insignificance of 'Significance': James, Kuhn, and Flyvbjerg." *Interactions: UCLA Journal of Education and Information Studies* 9 (2). http://escholarship.org/uc/item/2jr6h0k1.
St. Pierre E. A. 2011. "Post Qualitative Research: The Critique and the Coming After." In *SAGE Handbook of Qualitative Inquiry*. 4th ed., edited by Norman K. Denzin and Yvonna S. Lincoln, 611–25. Los Angeles: SAGE.
———. 2016. "Deleuze and Guattari's Language for New Empirical Inquiry." *Educational Philosophy and Theory* (June 7): 1–10. DOI: 10.1080/00131857.2016.1151761.

I would like to extend my thanks to Patti Lather for her critical remarks on an earlier version of this paper and to Elizabeth Adams St. Pierre for her generous dialogue and correspondence from which this chapter benefited greatly.

NOTE

1. For my particular critique of social science, see: Rocha, S. D. 2013. "Unscientific Science and the Insignificance of 'Significance': James, Kuhn, and Flyvbjerg." *Interactions: UCLA Journal of Education and Information Studies* 9 (2).

Chapter Twelve

The Blurring and Entanglement of Philosophy and Science

A Response

Patti Lather

> "Thou shalt not sit
> With statisticians nor commit
> A social science."

—W. H. Auden (quoted in Van Maanen, 1988, 13)

This response to Sam's chapter is framed by my relationship with him, particularly during his doctoral years at OSU where, while he took courses with me in feminist methodology and Foucault, he did not avail himself of the qualitative sequence I taught although, ironically, he ended up teaching such courses in one of his early jobs. This has been a running thread of teasing between us and serves, perhaps, as one of the subtexts of this paper.

To my mind, the object of Sam's critique is a conflation of social science, scientism, and science itself, sometimes writ large and sometimes its education variant, and how this impacts philosophy of education where his fierce disciplinary commitments lie. This is a commitment Sam surely shares with Dewey although Dewey's scientific agenda for education becomes part of the problem for Sam. "Balancing" his critique of Dewey with William James toward a more cautionary tale is well taken but, to my less than Dewey expert mind, still misses the boat.

Given the view of science at that time—what Sam later calls "the progressive faith in the power of science,"—Dewey's "scientific gusto" is, as Sam says, well known, and surely open to critique as long as recognized as of its time. Sam knows this to some degree. But where is the "Dewey versus

Thorndike" battle for dominance so powerfully captured in Eleanor Lagemann (1989)? What is missing in Sam's critique of Dewey's science has to do with the very context of Dewey's loss to Thorndike's psychometrics that were plenty "vulgar" at the time. Education research has long suffered the cost, and who is to blame is less the issue than what is to be done.

In regard to engagement with St. Pierre, any "return to philosophy" is grounded in how modern science began as "Natural Philosophy," a mix of philosophy, reason, and Enlightenment humanism. This troubles Sam's argument for the "pre-qualitative" status of philosophy. There is a return going on here, precisely, but it is, to use St. Pierre's words, to the entanglement of science and philosophy at its modern roots.

In more contemporary times, grounded in a distinction between science and scientism and an evocation of the sciences/humanities split, the "science wars" are pretty much driving St. Pierre. While Sam wants to keep the argument at the level of education, this larger context is too much a force to be left out.

Sam gets into this more deeply as the essay goes on, but again, the argument is set up against science as opposed to against SCIENTISM, and most importantly to me, the social science wrestling with itself over the last forty or more years is left out. Getting closer and closer to the humanities in that wrestling, Sam's phrase the "dogmatism of social scientific slumber" erases the complicated history of the social sciences as dominated by just these tensions between science, scientism, and the humanities/sciences split.

I had my qualitative students read Celine-Marie Pascale's *Cartographies of Knowledge* (2010) as but one example of this huge literature.[1] *Writing Culture: The Poetics and Politics of Ethnography* (1986) from anthropology is an early sign of the social sciences blurring into the humanities. It ripped the field of anthropology apart but in the intervening years has quite won the battle. Rather than "slumber" the social sciences have been characterized by this methodological/paradigmatic/philosophical fight, one could argue, ever since Kuhn's *The Structure of Scientific Revolutions* (1962). While taking some years to infuse into the social sciences, Kuhn's book is now deemed a classic in bringing history to the, in Kuhn's case, natural sciences. And I can't help but mention the "science studies" movement that has permeated philosophical, historical, and ethnographic readings of science (surely including social science) for the past thirty or more years, Donna Haraway (1991) being but one prime example. St. Pierre's work grows out of this tradition, now framed by Karen Barad (2007) and her work in quantum physics and the "new" materialisms.

I think where all of this ends up is undercutting the "pre" of Sam's concluding argument. Right, no one needs to die. But the various disciplinary perspectives have been blurring boundaries for quite some time now, of late evidencing in the "new humanities"[2] with its links to digital culture and science, including neuroscience, evolutionary biology, and the "new psychology." There is even a "neurohumanities" major recently debuted at Duke.

And there is even movement on the quantitative research front in education as evidenced in recent work I have undertaken with Elizabeth de Freitas and Ezekiel Dixon-Roman. As guest editors of a special (in press) issue of *Cultural Studies/Critical Methodologies*, we combined the history of mathematics, quantitative policy analysis, and qualitative research in education to look at what we came to call cultural studies of numeracy. Inspired by feminist work in the "new materialisms" (Barad 2007; Kirby 2011), we asked what this body of work might mean for social inquiry, especially its quantitative variants. Our search for contributors took us across digital and computational cultures, information science, measurement and assessment, forms of calculation, machine learning, and software thinking. Algorithmic thought especially kept popping up as an object of study but so did Google graphs, cybernetics, networks, "becoming-statistics," fractal calculations, and the racialized assemblages of control societies. As a qualitative methodologist, much of this was news to me, and I am surely the most outsider of the editorial group. But I have long been interested in shifts in the quantitative world that put philosophy to work in displacing the reign of psychometrics over education research.

As an example of such vanguard work in education, two educational philosophers, David Backer and Tyson Lewis (2015), aim to "rehabilitate" testing against the neoliberal framework of value using Avital Ronell's (2005) account of "the test drive." Ronell takes on the "overreaching claims to objectivity" (Backer and Lewis 2015, 197) of "the test drive" and offers an alternative genealogy in the context of a scientificity that, with its metaphysics, "would never submit to testing nor pass if it did" (198). Looking at how Pearson and other big businesses have profited from high-stakes testing through their "appropriation of scientific objectivity" (199), Backer and Lewis write of this "order of things": "Testing is an event that networks together law, education, science, and economy, creating an overarching regime wherein the guise of *science* justifies a depletion of the educative resources it is meant to enhance" (200). They foreground the learning that is unmeasurable within any matrices of paradigmatic forms of evaluation and assessment and urge experiments with "the test drive" that defy measurement and labeling by bringing aesthetic judgment to bear. They suggest building tests around "three operative logics" of health, taste, and personality in order to "suspend the entrepreneurial self" (206). This entails constructing new valences of what it means to be a subject, becoming otherwise than what neoliberalism demands.

All of this opens a next arena for critical work where philosophy is brought to bear in both pushing back on "the algorithm informational complex" and putting forward a social science far different from that alluded to by both Sam and W. H. Auden in the poem that opens this commentary.

To conclude, to leave Dewey may or may not be advisable and of course depends on the degree to which one buys into the binary Dewey as sketched by Sam—the bad science Dewey or the good philosophical Dewey. And I am not sure how any of this is to "precede" any other perspective as opposed to a "blurring" and entanglement that are much more the case.

Now if Sam had just taken those qualitative courses with me, he would have known this.

REFERENCES

Backer, David Isaac, and Tyson Edward Lewis. 2015. "Retaking the Test." *Educational Studies* 51 (3): 193–208.
Barad, Karen. 2007. *Meeting the Universe Half-Way*. Durham, NC: Duke University Press.
Clifford, James, and George Marcus, et al. 1986. *Writing Culture: The Poetics and Politics of Ethnography*. Berkeley: University of California Press.
Haraway, Donna. 1991. *Simians, Cyborgs and Women: The Reinvention of Nature*. New York: Routledge.
Kirby, Vicky. 2011. *Quantum Anthropologies: Life at Large*. Durham, NC: Duke University Press.
Kitchin, Rob. 2014. *The Data Revolution*. Los Angeles, CA: Sage.
Kuhn, Thomas B. 1962. *The Structure of Scientific Revolutions*. Chicago: University of Chicago Press.
Lagemann, Ellen. 1989. "The plural worlds of educational research." *History of Education Quarterly* 29 (2): 185–214.
Pascale, Celine-Marie. 2010. *Cartographies of Knowledge: Exploring Qualitative Epistemologies*. Thousand Oaks, CA: Sage.
Ronell, Avital. 2005. *The Test Drive*. Urbana: University of Illinois Press.
Van Maanen, John. 1988. *Tales of the Field: On Writing Ethnography*. Chicago: University of Chicago Press.

NOTES

1. See Patti Lather, 2013. "To Give Good Science," review of *Cartographies of Knowledge: Exploring Qualitative Epistemologies. Qualitative Studies in Education* 26 (6): 759–62.
2. This is a huge literature. For a particularly lively and visual look at the issues, see *The Point Newsletter*, especially issue 8, "What Is Science For?" See, also, chapter 8, "The Reframing of Science, Social Science and Humanities Research," of *The Data Revolution*, Rob Kitchin, 2014.

Index

ableism, 106
action-guiding scholarship, 76, 77, 79
Acuña, Rodolfo, 51, 56; *Occupied America*, 54
Africa, 104
Africana philosophy, 106
Alpha Report, 92
American Educational Research Association (AERA), 99
American Historical Society (AHA): Commission on the Social Studies, 39–40
American Psychological Association (APA), 32, 85n1, 126
analogical inference, 20
analytical philosophy, 75
anthropology, 103, 134
Anzaldúa, Gloria, 101
Aristotle, 14, 21, 22, 44
Auden, W. H., 133, 135

Backer, David, 135
Bacon, Francis, 14, 18, 22
Barad, Karen, 134
Beard, Charles Austin, 44
Beethoven, L., 45
behaviorism, 41
Bernasconi, Robert, 106
Beta Report, 92
Bigelow, Bill and Bob Peterson: *Rethinking Columbus*, 54

Blount, Jackie M., xvi, xvii, 18–19, 19–20, 143
Bobbitt, Franklin, 40
Bode, Boyd, xvi, 40, 41, 42, 48; *Conflicting Psychologies of Learning*. See *How We Learn*; *Fundamentals of Education*, 40; *How We Learn* 41; *Modern Educational Theories*, 40–41
borderlands, 101, 107
Boyle, Robert, 115
Brandt, Bettina, 103
Brayton, Laura, 36
Britzman, Deborah, 131
Buenos Aires, Argentina, 3–4, 5, 6, 11
Burke, Kenneth, 15
Burton, M. L., 67

Cartesian predicament, 105
Catlin, George, 58
Charters, W. W., 40
chemistry, 111, 112
Chicago School of Thought, 31
China, 104
Cicero, 6
civic education, 79, 82, 83
class struggle, 52, 55
Clastres, Pierre, 58, 59
Clifford, James, 102
cognitive science, 75
Cohen, Morris, 15
Colden, Cadwallader, 57

Columbia University, 28, 64
complex communication, xix, 102
Conant, James Bryant, xix, 23, 111–121;
    On Understanding Science, 115;
    Science and Common Sense, 115–116, 118, 119
concept as method, 130
conceptual binaries, 102–103
consciousness, 5, 6, 9, 40, 41, 42, 53; false, 101; historical, 6, 8, 15
Contributions to Education Series, xvi, 27–38
Council for Social Foundations of Education (CSFE), 39
Counts, George S., 7, 11; "Criteria for Judging a Philosophy of Education," 7–8; *The School and Society in Chicago*, 35; *The Social Foundations of Education*, 39–40
Critical Race Theory, 51, 56
critical theory, 131
Cultural Studies/Critical Methodologies, 135
Curren, Randall, x, xviii, 25n1, 80, 83, 85n1, 145
Curren, Randall and Charles Dorn, x, xviii; *Patriotic Education: Realizing America in a Global Age*, 83
curriculum theory, xvi, 124, 131

daimon, xv, 6, 10
Darwin, Charles, 20; *Origin of Species*, 18
deduction, xiii, 9, 10, 14–15, 17, 21, 116, 117; ethico-historical, 8, 9; as scientific method, 14
de Freitas, Elizabeth, 135
Delgado, Richard and Jean Stefancic: *Critical Race Theory*, 51, 56
democratic: citizenship, 82, 113; threshold, 9
Descartes, René, 105
Dewey, Alice, 30, 38n1
Dewey, John, xiv, xvi, xviii, 6, 21, 22, 27–38, 41, 42, 46, 124–127, 127–128, 129, 130, 131, 133–134, 136; *Art as Experience*, 126; as teacher, 29; Center for Dewey Studies, 29; *Democracy and Education*, 28, 126; "Education as a University Study," 125; "Pedagogy as a University Discipline," 125; *Psychology and Social Practice*, 32; "Social Science and Social Control," 126; *The Child and the Curriculum*, 34; *The Educational Situation*, 32–33
disabilities: individuals with, 106
disappeared people, xvii, xix, 3, 99–110
Dixon-Roman, Ezekiel, 135
Dorn, Charles, xviii, 82, 83, 145
double consciousness, 101, 108; white, xix
Douglas, Diane, 53
DuBois, W. E. B., 101

Edel, Abraham, 75, 76
Einstein, Albert, 41
Eliot, Charles W., 63, 63–64, 65–66, 66, 69, 70
empiricism, 14, 130
endowment, university, xvii, 63, 64–65, 65, 67, 68
Enlightenment, 42, 54, 103, 104, 106, 107, 134; German, 103
epagoge, 21
epistemic decolonization, 108
epistemic liberation, 108
equality, 9–10, 57, 60, 88, 90, 93
erasure, xvi, xx, 56, 100, 101, 105
eros, 6
Errante, Antoinette, xix, 143
Escuela Superior de Mecánica de la Armada. *See* Naval Mechanics School
ethnicity, 53, 56
ethnography, 101, 134
Eze, Emmanuel, 104

Falk, Thomas, xvi, xvii, 145
feminist: historians, 106; methodology, 133; philosophy, 75; research, 135; studies, xiv
Fitzgerald, F. Scott: *The Great Gatsby*, 46
Foucault, Michel, 15, 133
Franklin, Benjamin, 43, 46
free-money ideology, xvii, 63, 63–64, 66, 68, 69, 70
Freire, Paulo, 131; *Pedagogy of the Oppressed*, 51, 52
Frye, Northrup, 15
Fullen, John B., 67

Gamma Report, 92
Geertz, Clifford, 17
general education, 112–113, 113, 115, 119, 120
Greene, Maxine, xvi, 40, 43–44, 45–48, 131; *Landscapes of Learning*, 46–47; "Releasing the Imagination," 47; *The Dialectic of Freedom*, 47–48; *The Public School and the Private Vision*, 43, 45–46
Grumet, Madeline, 131
Gutmann, Amy, 9

Haley, Margaret, 29
Haraway, Donna, 134
Harper, William Rainey, 28, 29, 30
Harvard University, 23, 63, 64, 65–66, 66, 111, 112, 115, 116, 119, 120, 128; Endowment Fund Campaign, 63, 64, 66; Harvard College, 112, 113; Harvard Committee on General Education, 113; president, 111, 119
Haymes, Stephen, 106, 107
Hegel, Georg Wilhelm Friedrich, 104
Heidegger, Martin, 75
Herschel, F. W., 19
Hibben, John, 66
History and Philosophy Series, 77
History of Education Society (HES), 80, 85n1
history of science, xix, 23, 111–112, 113, 114, 118, 119, 134
Hobsbawm, Eric, 53
Hofstadter, Richard: *Anti-intellectualism in American Life*, 43
Horne, Tom, 52
human variation, 103, 105
humanities, xiii, xv, xvii, xx, 39, 112, 126, 130, 131, 134
Huppenthal, John, 52
hypothesis, 17, 22–23, 23, 34, 78, 114, 116
hypothetico-deductive reasoning, 17

ideal theory, 77
identity group, 87, 92
Illich, Ivan, 123
IMPACT pamphlet series, 80, 85n2
imperialism, 52

indigenous: Americans, xvii, 54, 57; people, xiii, 56; traditions, xvii
individualism, 43, 46
induction, xiii, xv, 14–15, 17–18, 19, 20, 21, 22, 23; analogical, 19, 19–20, 21; enumerative, xv, 18, 19, 20, 21; inductive verification, 19, 19–20; intuitive. *See* epagoge; inventive, 22, 23, 24; is ampliative, 20; type, 21, 22, 23, 24
Infeld, Leopold, 41
intuition, xiii, xiv–xv, 23, 44, 88, 116, 117; historical, 9–11
invisibility. *See* erasure
Iowa State University, 69
Isaac, Joel, 119–120
Isocrates, 44, 45

James, William, x, 4–5, 5–6, 31, 125, 126, 127–128, 131, 132n1, 133; Jamesean blindness, xv, 4–5, 5–6, 7, 10; *Talks to Teachers on Psychology*, 127
Jefferson, Thomas, 46
Johnson, Benjamin, xvi–xvii, 145
justice, xviii, 77, 78, 87, 88, 91, 93, 94, 95, 96, 96–97; injustice, 4, 77, 88, 96; social justice, 10, 42

Kant, Immanuel, 104
Kilpatrick, William Heard: project method, 40
Kimball, Bruce, xv, xix, 143
Kuhn, Thomas S., xix–xx, xx, 15, 19, 23, 120, 132n1; *The Structure of Scientific Revolutions*, 23, 120, 134

Laboratory School, 28, 29–30, 38n1, 126, 126–8, 128
Lagemann, Ellen Condliffe, 28, 134
Lather, Patti, xv, xx, 131, 132, 136n1, 146
Latino students, 51, 52, 52–53, 54, 60
Lazarus, Eli, 81, 82
Le Jeune, Paul, 57
Levi-Strauss, Claude, 58
Lewis, Tyson, 135
LGBTQ people, 106, 108
liberal arts, 45, 113, 118
liberalism, ix, xviii, 87, 88–92, 93–96, 96–97, 97n3, 98n6, 98n8;

neoliberalism, xx, 135
liberty, 57, 60, 88, 90, 93
Lincoln, James F., 67
Lindeman, Eduard, 64
linguistic turn, 16, 17, 100
literature, xiv, xv, xvi, xix, 13, 14, 15, 16, 18, 23, 24, 30, 40, 44, 45–46, 48, 52, 75, 131
Locke, John, 41
Lugones, María, xix, 102, 107, 108

Manifest Destiny, 52
Mann, Charles, 57
Mann, Horace, 45
Mannheim, Karl, 15
Martin, Jane Roland: *Reclaiming a Conversation*, 36
Martinez, Jacqueline, 100
Marx, Karl, 75
Marxism, 52
McManis, John, 35
Mehl, Bernard, xvi, 40, 42–45, 48; *Classical Educational Ideas*, 43, 44–45; educational imagination, 43
Melville, Herman, 46
Mesoamerican civilizations, xvii, 51, 54, 56, 57
Mexican American students, 53, 60
Mexican American Studies Program (MASP), xvii, 51, 52, 52–53, 54–55, 55, 56, 57, 59
Michigan State University, 69
Michigan, University of, 38n1, 66, 67–68, 69–70
Mill, John Stuart, 14, 19, 19–20, 20, 21, 22, 22–23
Miller, Sue: *The Good Mother*, 48
Mills, Charles, 98n7, 105
Morrill Land-Grant Act, 69
Morrill, James L., 67
Morrison, Toni, 47
Mozambicans, 100–101, 101
multiculturalism, 47

Nagel, Ernest, 15
narrative turn. *See* linguistic turn
Nasruddin, 59
National Education Association (NEA), 28
National Research Council (NRC), 128

National Science Foundation (NSF), 119
nationalism, 55, 59
natural science, xv, xvii, xix, 14, 18, 77, 112, 113, 115, 117, 120, 126, 130, 134
Natural Science 4, 113, 120
Naval Mechanics School, 4, 6
Nietzsche, Friedrich, 75
Noddings, Nel, 131
non-ideal theory, 77, 77–78, 78, 78–79, 79
normative philosophy, 96
normative political theory, 77

Ohio State University, The, xvii, 21, 63, 66, 67, 68, 69, 70, 129, 133; Association, 67; Development Fund, 68
Orwell, George, 55
Outlaw, Lucius, 103

paradigm, 23, 77, 79, 134, 135
Pascale, Celine-Marie: *Cartographies of Knowledge*, 134
patriotism, xviii, 79, 81–82, 82, 83
Peirce, Charles, 20, 21, 23
phenomenology, 17, 46–47
philosopher's stone, 103, 104
Pinar, William, 131
Plato, 6, 44
Pledge of Allegiance, 82
pluralism, 43, 44, 47
positivism, x, 17, 128
post qualitative inquiry, 124, 128–129, 129–130, 130
postmodernism, 128, 129
post-structuralism, 129, 130
Poynter Center for the Study of Ethics and American Institutions, 79
practical philosophy, 76, 80, 83
pragmatism, 35, 41, 46, 75, 126
predicament of culture, 102, 105
presentism, 83
Princeton University, 65–66
Pritchett, Henry, 64
psychology, xx, 30, 32, 35, 41, 125–127, 127–128; moral, 75; new, 134; psychologists, xvi, 40, 41, 75, 125, 126, 127–128; social, 117, 126
psychometrics, 134, 135; applied, 126; educational, xx, 75; psychometricians, 75–76, 124

Purdy, Daniel, 103
Puritanism, 42–43; Puritans, 46

quace, xviii, 91–92, 92, 93, 94, 97, 98n7, 98n9
qualitative research, xx, 124, 128–129, 131, 133, 134, 135, 136
Quine-Duhem thesis, 9

race, ix, 51, 53, 56, 93–95, 95–96, 97, 98n6, 98n9, 103–104
racism, 45, 55, 59, 106
Rawls, John, 77; *A Theory of Justice*, 77
reconciliation, xix, 102, 106, 108
relativism, 16, 17, 22
Rightmire, George W., xvii, 63, 66–67, 68, 70
Robertson, Emily, x
Rocha, Sam, xv, xx, 132n1, 133–134, 134, 135, 136, 146
Rogers, Robert, 57
Ronell, Avital, 135
Rorty, Richard, 103, 104–105
Rosales, Arturo and Francisco Rosales: *Chicano! The History of the Mexican Civil Rights Movement*, 54

SAGE Handbook of Qualitative Inquiry, 128
Sanchez, H. T., 52, 53
science education, xix, 111, 114, 119
scientific inquiry, 22, 34
scientific method, xix, 14–18, 23, 34, 111, 114, 116, 118
sexism, 106
slavery, 103
Snedden, David, 40
social foundations of education, xvi
social sciences, xiii, xiv, xvii, xix, xx, 18, 39, 78, 111, 112, 113, 115, 117, 117–118, 118–119, 120, 124, 126, 127–128, 128, 129, 130, 131, 132n1, 133, 134, 135, 136n2
Socrates, 6
South Africans, 100

Spongberg, Mary, 106, 107
St. Pierre, Elizabeth Adams, xx, 124, 128–131, 132, 134
Swift, Adam, 78

Tartaglia, James, 104
Thompson, Winston C., xviii, 146
Thorndike, Edward Lee, xx, 41, 134
Tucson Unified School District, xvii, 51
Turner, Frederick Jackson, 44
Tutu, Desmond, 108
Twain, Mark, 48

Urban, Wayne, xix, 23, 146

Warnick, Bryan, x, xv, 25n1, 79, 147
Watras, Joe, xvi, 147
Wechsler, Harold, 80, 85n1
Wever, Sarah, xix, 147
Whewell, William, 14, 20, 21, 22–23
white supremacy, 52
White, Hayden, 15, 22; *Metahistory*, 15–16, 16–17, 23
Winship, A. E., 31
Wolf, Eric, 52
women, 15, 27, 29, 30, 30–31, 36, 48, 99, 101, 106
Writing Culture: The Poetics and Politics of Ethnography, 134

Yacek, Doug, 25n2
Yale University, 64, 65–66, 118
Yancy, George, xix, 101, 105, 108
Young, Ella Flagg, xvi, 27–38; as dropout from school, 30; Dewey compares to Theodore Roosevelt 35; *Ethics in the School*, 33; *Isolation in the School*, 29, 31–32, 32, 33; *Some Types of Educational Theory*, 34

Zimmerman, Jonathan, ix–xi, xviii, 79, 80, 85n1
Zinn, Howard, 53–54
Žižek, Slavoj, 55

About the Editors

Antoinette Errante is associate professor of educational studies at Ohio State University. She has published articles in the *American Journal of Education, Educational Researcher, Comparative Education Review, Paedagogica Historica, História de Educação* (Brazil), and the *International Journal of African Historical Studies* on oral history methodology, Lusophone colonial educational history, and trauma, healing, and conflict transformation as cultural practices.

Jackie M. Blount is professor of educational studies at Ohio State University. She has written *Destined to Rule the Schools: Women and the Superintendency, 1873–1995* (SUNY Press, 1998) and *Fit to Teach: Same-Sex Desire, Gender, and School Work in the Twentieth Century* (SUNY Press, 2005) and coauthored *Radicalizing Educational Leadership: The Dimensions of Social Justice* (Sense Publishing, 2008). Her work has been published in such journals as *Harvard Educational Review, Educational Administration Quarterly,* and *Review of Educational Research*. Currently, she is president-elect of the History of Education Society.

Bruce Kimball is professor of educational studies at Ohio State University and a former Guggenheim fellow. He is the author or coauthor of *On the Battlefield of Merit: Harvard Law School in the First Century* (Harvard, 2015), *The Inception of Modern Professional Education* (University of North Carolina, 2009), *The Condition of American Liberal Education: Pragmatism and a Changing Tradition* (College Board, 1995), *The "True Professional Ideal" in America: A History* (Blackwell, 1992), *Orators and Philosophers: A History of the Idea of Liberal Education* (Teachers College Press, 1986).

About the Contributors

Randall Curren was professor at the Royal Institute of Philosophy (London) and chair of Moral and Virtue Education at the University of Birmingham (England) from 2013 to 2015. During 2012–2013, he held a fellowship at the Institute for Advanced Study in Princeton. Among his books are *Philosophy of Education: An Anthology* (Blackwell, 2007), *A Companion to the Philosophy of Education* (Blackwell, 2003), and *Aristotle on the Necessity of Public Education* (Rowman & Littlefield, 2000). He is one of the two coeditors of the History and Philosophy of Education book series of the University of Chicago Press.

Charles Dorn is associate dean for academic affairs and professor of education at Bowdoin College. His work has appeared in the *American Journal of Education*, *Diplomatic History*, *Teachers College Record*, and *History of Education Quarterly*. He is the author of *American Education, Democracy, and the Second World War* (Palgrave Macmillan, 2007) and *For the Common Good: A New History of Higher Education in America* (forthcoming from Cornell University Press).

Thomas M. Falk received his PhD in philosophy of education from Ohio State University in 2012. He currently teaches at the University of Dayton and writes in the areas of critical theory, phenomenology, and cultural and intellectual history.

Benjamin Johnson is an assistant professor of student leadership and success studies at Utah Valley University. His research interests include higher education leadership, student metacognition, faculty-student mentoring, history and philosophy of education, and comparative and international education.

He has authored or coauthored articles in *Comparative and International Higher Education, Teachers College Record, History of Education Quarterly, Philosophical Studies in Education,* and *Educational Theory.*

Patti Lather is professor emerita in the School of Educational Studies at the Ohio State University, where she taught qualitative research, feminist methodology, and gender and education since 1988. She is the author of five books, *Getting Smart: Feminist Research and Pedagogy with/in the Postmodern* (1991 Critics Choice Award), *Troubling the Angels: Women Living with HIV/AIDS,* coauthored with Chris Smithies (1998 CHOICE Outstanding Academic Title), *Getting Lost: Feminist Efforts toward a Double(d) Science* (2008 Critics Choice Award), and *Engaging (Social) Science: Policy from the Side of the Messy* (2011 Critics Choice Award), and *(Post)Critical Methodologies: The Science Possible after the Critiques: The Selected Writings of Patti Lather,* in press. She was the recipient of a 1989 Fulbright to New Zealand. She is a 2009 inductee of the AERA Fellows and a 2010 recipient of the AERA Division B Lifetime Achievement Award.

Sam Rocha is the author of *A Primer for Philosophy and Education* (Pickwick, 2014.) He has published essays on ethics, democracy, folk culture, and other subjects in *Educational Philosophy and Theory, Lapíz: Journal of the Latin American Philosophy of Education Society, Philosophy of Education, InterActions: UCLA Journal of Education and Information Studies, Studies in Philosophy and Education, Philosophical Studies in Education,* and *Educational Theory.*

Winston C. Thompson is an assistant professor in the Department of Education and affiliate faculty in the Department of Philosophy at the University of New Hampshire. He received his PhD in philosophy of education from Teachers College, Columbia University. Thompson's scholarship focuses upon normative ethical and social/political questions of justice, race, education, and the public good, with recent efforts analyzing dilemmas of educational policy. Thompson is currently working on detailing the relationship between education and politics under liberalism. He has published articles in the *Journal of Educational Controversy, Educational Theory, Philosophy and Education,* and *Democracy and Education.*

Wayne Urban is past president of the History of Education Society and author of *American Education: A History* (Routledge, 2014), *More than Science and Sputnik: The National Defense Education Act of 1958* (University of Alabama Press, 2010), *Gender, Race, and the National Education Association: Professionalism and Its Limitations* (Falmer, 2000), *Black Scholar: Horace Mann Bond, 1904–1972* (University of Georgia Press,

1992), *Why Teachers Organized* (Wayne State University Press, 1982), and other books.

Bryan Warnick is professor of philosophy of education at the Ohio State University. Current chair of the AERA Philosophical Studies in Education SIG, Warnick is the author of *Understanding Student Rights in Schools: Speech, Privacy, and Religion in Educational Contexts* (Teachers College Press, 2012) and *Imitation and Education: A Philosophical Inquiry into Learning by Example* (SUNY Press, 2008). His essays have appeared in *Educational Theory*, *Teachers College Record*, and *Harvard Educational Review*.

Joe Watras was professor of history and philosophy of education at the University of Dayton. He was the author of *Philosophies of Environmental Education and Democracy: Harris, Dewey, and Bateson on Human Freedoms in Nature* (Palgrave Macmillan, 2015), *A History of American Education* (Allyn and Bacon, 2008), *Philosophical Conflicts in Education, 1893–2000* (Allyn and Bacon, 2004), *The Foundations of Educational Curriculum and Diversity, 1565 to the Present* (Allyn and Bacon, 2002), and *Politics, Race, and Schools: Racial Integration, 1954–1994* (Garland, 1997). He is also author of numerous scholarly articles, including his essay "Education for Environmental Protection: The Story and the Resources," which was published in the July 2016 issue of *CHOICE: Current Reviews for Academic Libraries*.

Sarah Wever is a PhD student in the higher education administration program at the University of Alabama. She is currently studying university presidents and leaders in the South and how they handled the desegregation of their universities. She has done extensive research on Oliver Carmichael and Autherine Lucy.

www.ingramcontent.com/pod-product-compliance
Lightning Source LLC
Chambersburg PA
CBHW020740230426
43665CB00009B/506